# Middle Eastern Home Cooking

Quick, easy, delicious recipes to make at home

# Middle Eastern Home Cooking

## TESS MALLOS

PERIPLUS

First published in the United States in 2002 by Periplus Editions (HK) Ltd.,
with editorial offices at 153 Milk Street, Boston, Massachusetts 02109
and 130 Joo Seng Road #06-01/03 Singapore 368357

Library of Congress Cataloging-in-Publication Data is available.
ISBN 0-7946-5014-7

DISTRIBUTED BY

North America, Latin America,
and Europe
Tuttle Publishing
Distribution Center
Airport Industrial Park
364 Innovation Drive
North Clarendon, VT 05759-9436
Tel: (802) 773-8930
Tel: (800) 526-2778

Japan and Korea
Tuttle Publishing
Yaekari Building, 3rd Floor
5-4-12 Osaki, Shinagawa-ku
Tokyo 141 0032
Tel: (03) 5437-0171
Fax: (03) 5437-0755

Asia Pacific
Berkeley Books Pte. Ltd.
130 Joo Seng Road
#06-01/03
Singapore 368357
Tel: (65) 6280-3320
Fax: (65) 6280-6290

Commissioned by Deborah Nixon
Text: Tess Mallos
Photographer & Stylist: Vicki Liley
Designer: Robyn Latimer
Editor: Judith Dunham
Production Manager: Sally Stokes
Project Coordinator: Rea Hatzi-Fatouros

First Edition
06 05 04 03 02 01   10 9 8 7 6 5 4 3 2 1

3 2530 60559 8/90

Set in Spartan Classified on QuarkXPress
Printed in Singapore

Cover image: Orange Rice with Chicken, page 67
Page 2: Chickpea and Sesame Puree, page 34
Page 3: Beet with Garlic Sauce, page 48
Opposite: Skewered Grilled Chicken, page 64

641.5956
MALL

# Contents

# Introduction

When I was researching Middle Eastern cooking in many of the countries of the region, I had the opportunity to learn from many good home cooks. There were a number of foods and dishes similar to the Greek cuisine I know intimately, but I also learned how to stabilize yogurt, different and exciting ways to cook rice, the intricacies involved in making a good kibbe, and how to use a wider variety of herbs and spices. Once I became more familiar with the ingredients and techniques involved, it didn't take long to master Middle Eastern cooking.

I added my own skills to this new-found knowledge so that the recipes would be easier to follow in the kitchens of the uninitiated. Since many home cooks are strapped for time, this book offers less complicated and time-consuming versions for several recipes. See, for example, the recipes for Kibbe (page 80) and Falafel (page 33) the ground chickpea patties of Lebanon and Syria. Those familiar with the dish may wonder why the recipe here does not call for the dried fava beans traditionally used with the chickpeas; but falafel from chickpeas only is known in the region, and this version saves the home cook from having to soak the dried fava beans for two days and then painstakingly remove the tough skins before grinding the beans.

In the past, considerable manual labor was involved in Middle Eastern cooking, and this remains so in the villages of the region. However, modern cooks living in cities, and particularly in Western cities, make use of labor-saving appliances whenever possible. Kibbe was once painstakingly pounded in a large mortar with a pestle, or the meat was passed through a manually operated meat grinder. It is now likely to be ground in an electric-powered grinder or,

better still, "pounded" in a food processor, the latter an invaluable tool for preparing many of the region's dishes. An Iranian cook I met used an electric rice cooker; however, I still prefer the traditional method for the wonderful Iranian chelou – Steamed Rice (page 103) – especially when I want it crispy and golden brown on the bottom.

Cooking a cuisine at home far away from its origins can present some difficulties, as special ingredients may occasionally be needed. However, Middle Eastern markets are now found in many cities, and the special ingredients used in this book can usually be obtained there. Health food stores also stock many of the foods required. In some recipes I have suggested easily available ingredients as substitutes for those that may be difficult to locate. The Ingredients section (page 14) and the Glossary (page 120) list important ingredients, and contain instructions for making spice blends and clarified butter.

### A region stretching back to antiquity

The recipes in this book cover an area that stretches from Turkey in the west to Afghanistan in the east and from Armenia in the north to Egypt and Yemen in the south; it also includes the island of Cyprus, which is part Greek and part Turkish. What is called the Middle East today is a region stretching back to antiquity, with cultures and religions that reflect its colorful history. Yet its cuisine is very much a cuisine of today, with natural foods such as cereal grains, dried beans, nuts, yogurt, vegetables and fruits regarded as important components of a healthy diet. The pool of recipes for the region is vast, and it was difficult to make choices for this book. Many recipes, such as Koupepia (Stuffed Grapevine Leaves, page 30), Hummus bi Tahini (Chickpea and

Sesame Puree, page 34) and Tabbouleh (Bulgur and Parsley Salad, page 43), are included because they are well-known. Others such as Basal Mahshi (Stuffed Onions, page 72), Oktapothi Stifatho (Braised Octopus and Onions, page 51) and Baqlawa (Almond Baklava, page 115) were selected for their appeal to adventurous cooks. Whatever dish you choose to prepare, it will make a memorable contribution to your table.

## History of the region

No other region in the world has such a rich and varied history as the Middle East. It is within this region that the earliest civilizations, the Sumerian civilization of Mesopotamia (in present-day Iraq) and the Egyptian, took root and flourished from 3000 BC onward. The Empires of Babylonia, Assyria and Persia significantly influenced the region's development, as did Alexander the Great (Hellenistic Period) and other groups such as the Phoenicians and Hebrews of the Levant (Eastern Mediterranean), the Ancient Greeks and Romans, and the Parthians.

But the story starts 4000 years earlier. From about 7000 BC, humans began to control their food supply by cultivating wild wheat, barley and millet, and domesticating wild sheep, goats and cattle. It is thought these practices began in the valleys of the Zagros mountains of Iran and the Fertile Crescent, an area of land curving from the Eastern Mediterranean to the head of the Persian Gulf, encompassing the Tigris and Euphrates rivers. These waterways allowed irrigation of crops, and the settlements that grew around the cultivated areas developed eventually into the beginnings of the early civilizations.

## The culinary melting pot

With the passage of time, Egyptian, Persian, Hellenistic and Roman influences would blend, forming a varied yet distinctive Middle Eastern cuisine. The foods available in the region gave the cuisine its framework. These were cooked using the basic methods of broiling (grilling), roasting, frying and boiling, but there was also much experimentation, especially in the kitchens of the ruling class and the wealthy. The numerous ingredients available and those introduced through conquest were all used in these culinary experiments.

Books on cookery were written during the Hellenistic era, but only titles and excerpts survive in other works, especially in *Philosophers at Dinner*, by Athenaeus (c. 200 AD). One excerpt quoted in this work is relevant to the cooking of the region today; it originally appeared in *The Life of Luxury*, (c. 330 BC), written by Archestratus, a Sicilian Greek gastronome who ate and wrote his way from Sicily to Lydia (Asia Minor):

"... All those other tragemata (foods served with wine) are a sign of wretched poverty: boiled chickpeas, fava beans, apples and dried figs."

Yet it is the foods of the underprivileged that have remained static in the region, perhaps with a new seasoning or two added. The Shourba Ads (Red Lentil Soup, page 40) of Egypt, the Adas Bis Silq (Lentil and Swiss Chard Soup, page 38) and Falafel (Chickpea Patties, page 33) of Lebanon, Syria and Jordan, and the Nivik (Chickpeas with Spinach, page 96) of Armenia – all of these could well have been prepared since antiquity with ingredients indigenous to the region: lentils, chickpeas, garlic, onion, olive oil, chard, spinach, cumin and coriander. They would have been far more appealing than "... the belly and boiled womb of a sow in cumin and sharp vinegar and silphium" preferred by Archestratus. Silphium was a popular seasoning in Ancient Greece and Rome, a resin similar to asafoetida, used so widely that the plant from which it was obtained became extinct.

In 284 AD the Roman Empire was divided into western and eastern regions. By 330 AD, Rome's first Christian emperor, Constantine I, had built on

the Bosphorus his eponymous city. Constantinople was to become the heart of the Byzantine Empire after the collapse of the Roman Empire in 476 AD. Byzantium was to survive for 11 centuries, becoming the center for the Eastern Orthodox Church.

With a population made up of Greeks, Armenians, Italians and Syrians, Byzantium's cuisine developed from Hellenistic and Roman influences. Grapevine leaves replaced the brine-pickled fig leaves of Classical Greece for wrapping foods. The lavish use of olive oil characterized many of the foods, especially in the vegetable and pulse dishes required for the many fasting days of the Christian faith; Aginares me Koukia (Artichokes with Fava Beans, page 87) from Cyprus is typical. Lentil soup and fava (a puree of boiled split peas) are also still eaten today. Saffron was used in cooking, where previously it had been used to flavor wine. Feta cheese and the mild-flavored white cheese originated in Byzantium. The Byzantines excelled in fruit preserves too, from quince, pear and citron, and they made flavored non-alcoholic drinks especially for fast days using mastic, aniseed and rose. The Persians were responsible for introducing sugar to the region from India, creating a refining process in the 5th century AD. This aided the wider development of sweet foods and beverages.

However, the most important early influence on Middle Eastern food came from the Sassanian Persian Empire. After the end of Alexander the Great's short-lived Empire, and the decline of Parthian rule in Persia, the Sassanids came to power in 226 AD, determined to restore the Persian Empire of Classical times that had encompassed the whole region and part of India (550–330 BC). This they accomplished in part, and an era of great prosperity began, centered in Ctesiphon, on the eastern bank of the Tigris River in present-day Iraq. Persian culture continued to develop to a high degree, along with the foods prepared in the courts of the Sassanid kings.

Dishes served in the court of Khosru II, the penultimate ruler of this empire (590–628 AD), have counterparts in the region's cooking today: meat marinated in yogurt with spices (the Kabaub of Afghanistan, page 73); a rice pudding including milk, eggs, honey and sugar (Muhallabia, page 109); stuffed vine leaves, of which many versions exist today, such as the Koupepia of Cyprus (page 30); and almond pastries flavored with spices, which could have been an early version of the Baqlawa of Iran (page 115).

Such was the cuisine at the time of the Arab conquests. It was in 637 AD, three years after the death of the prophet Muhammad, that the Arabs, fired with the zeal of Islam, conquered what is today's Iraq, followed by Syria, Egypt and Persia. The Arabs had food traditions of Bedouin origin – camel, goat or sheep's milk, ghee, dates, flat bread, and on occasion mutton, camel or game. The two cultures merged, with Persians converting to Islam, and the Arabs absorbing Persian culture, including their foods.

In 762, the Abbasid caliph, Mansur, laid the foundations of the new city of Baghdad on the west bank of the Tigris, relocating the Caliphate from Damascus. Thus began an era of great cultural development and learning, passing into legend as the time of the Thousand and One Arabian Nights. Over the next two centuries the courts of the caliphs became known for their splendor and the luxury of their table, with the Persian influence continuing. There were the sweet-sour flavors loved by the Persians, in the form of fruit with meats and poultry, such as the Hamuth Heloo (Lamb with Dried Fruit, page 79) of Iraq, sauces thickened with pounded nuts such as the Skorthalia (Garlic Sauce, page 48) of Cyprus, and foods introduced by the Persians to the region from both Classical and modern times, including saffron, rosewater and pomegranate. Rice had been introduced via the Silk Road from India in Classical times, with eggplant introduced in about the 5th century AD.

While the region had its indigenous spices – cumin, coriander seed, saffron, sumac and fenugreek – fragrant spices became increasingly important in cooking during this period. Arab traders had been active from ancient times, sailing from the Persian Gulf to India for supplies, or using land routes. Cassia cinnamon had come from China via the Silk Road, cardamom and pepper from India, and cinnamon, cloves and nutmeg from the Spice Islands of Indonesia, obtained by Indian merchants. Fragrant spices had first been used as incense and for perfumes, and during the years of the Roman Empire the Romans had also joined the trade, by sea from Alexandria, and via the Silk Road.

When Baghdad fell to the Selzuk Turks in the 11th century, and then the Ottoman Turks two centuries later, the city's inhabitants also adopted much of the Persian culture that was still evident in the courts of the caliphs. By 1435 the Ottoman Turks had taken Constantinople, and made it the capital of their Empire. Yet another era in the development of the region's cuisine began, building on Persian–Arabic–Byzantine influences. Each of these eras influenced food habits, creating in the various areas of the region cuisines that are a reflection of the historical and cultural ebb and flow.

With the discovery of the New World, chili and sweet peppers, tomatoes, potatoes, new legumes and various types of squash were eagerly adopted, and added new dimensions to existing cuisines. These new additions eventually reached the Middle East.

**Early culinary developments**

If you have a heavy stone mortar and pestle, you are using one of the world's oldest cooking appliances, dating back to prehistoric times. The mortar and pestle were used initially to pulverize grains, but this use was later extended to pulverizing nuts, spices and meats.

Transforming cereal grains into food was a long process for early humans. The grains were difficult to thresh, and had to be heated to make the coating of chaff and bran brittle enough to remove. This process cooked the grain. An edible porridge could be made from the pounded wheat or barley; cooled and shaped into a flat cake, it could also be cooked on hot stones. This early flatbread was edible while hot, but very hard when cold. It was not until the Egyptians had produced a strain of wheat that could be threshed without heating that breads became edible. Leavened bread was produced next, again in Egypt, and the secret of its preparation was zealously guarded for many decades. Today bread is the most important food throughout the region. Baked in traditional bread ovens or the tandoor, it is offered at every meal.

This early experimentation led to the development of bulgur wheat (Burghal). Once the heated grain was threshed and cracked, soaking in water softened the grain and made it edible, without further cooking if necessary. Bulgur must be one of the earliest "manufactured" foods, dating back some 4000 years

to the civilizations of Mesopotamia – 3500-539 BC (Sumer, Babylon and Assyria). Nowadays it is used in Syria, Lebanon, Iraq, Armenia, Turkey and Cyprus, and has also been adopted by the Gulf States.

**Customs and celebrations**

The diverse religions of the region continue to influence food habits. Followers of the Coptic Church in Egypt and the Eastern Orthodox faith in Armenia and Greek Cyprus, and to a lesser extent in Turkey, Lebanon and Syria, have their most important period of religious observance at Easter. The forty days of Lent is a time of fasting, when no animal foods are used. The Resurrection is celebrated on Easter Saturday evening, and then the fast is broken after midnight. The main celebration is held on Easter Sunday. Foods served vary according to the nationality of the celebrants, but dyed or painted boiled eggs, sweet Easter breads and roasted lamb feature in most celebrations in the region.

The one period in the Muslim year when fasting is mandatory is the month of Ramadan, commemorating the first revelation of the Koran. From daybreak to dusk, no food or beverage, including water, is allowed; only soldiers, the sick and pregnant women are exempt. The first meal of the day is taken before daybreak, usually in the form of leftovers from the night before. At sunset, the fast is broken with a drink of water and something sweet before attending prayers. The main meal is then taken, often with relatives and friends. Dishes served during Ramadan vary from country to country.

According to Islamic laws, animals must be humanely slaughtered facing Mecca, as the slaughterer utters the phrase: "In the name of God; God is most great." Thus the meat becomes lawful (halal). Pork is the only prohibited meat. Before and after meals, hands are ritually washed. While cutlery is widely used today, in many villages and at traditional feasts food is eaten by hand. Only the right hand is used, to pick up the food elegantly with the thumb and first two fingers; the left hand should not come into contact with food. Wine is forbidden, and while some countries forbid any alcoholic beverage, others allow beer and raki or arak (aniseed-flavored spirits), depending on the interpretation of the Koran.

Though Iran is predominantly a Muslim country, Now Rooz (New Year), its most joyous celebration, had its origins long before Islam. Now Rooz, a Spring festival, is Zoroastrian in origin, dating back to the great kings of the ancient Persian Empire. It begins on the first day of Spring, March 21, and lasts for 14 days. On Now Rooz eve, the haft seen (seven S's) table is set with seven items beginning with 's': sib (apple), sir (garlic), sumac, sabzi (herbs), sarkh (vinegar), sekeh (a coin) and samanoo, a sweet pudding made with a special wheat. Other raw foods are placed on the table, and these are used through-out the holiday period.

Hospitality in the region is frequently expressed with the offering of mezze, a variety of appetizers limited only by the availability of ingredients and the capacity of the cook to prepare them. Mezze comes from the Persian 'maza', meaning 'to taste or relish.' Arab hospitality is legendary: any visitor who calls in, even a stranger, is offered something to eat and drink. If it is meal-time, the visitor is invited to stay. Meals are always prepared in sufficient quantity for this eventuality.

**Serving a Middle Eastern meal**
In the traditional manner the meal is set out on a cloth-covered carpet, with diners sitting around it on cushions. Food is also typically served on a low table consisting of a large, intricately worked brass or copper tray supported by a tambour, a circular frame, or a wooden trestle; cushions are used for seating. In cities and larger towns, the meal may be served on a table in the Western manner. In some city households, there is often a dining area set up in the traditional manner, as well as one with Western furnishings and settings.

As a general rule, the food is served in large platters and bowls, with all the dishes of the meal placed on the table together at the beginning of the meal: soup (if served), the main course, pickles, salads, vegetable dishes, bowls of yogurt, bread, and jugs of water or yogurt drink. Pudding and/or fruit completes the meal.

Coffee is the beverage of choice in most of the region, although tea is also served, hot and sweet, in tea glasses. In the Gulf States certain protocol is observed when drinking coffee (see page 119). Tea is the preferred beverage in Iran, where the samovar is ever present. In Afghanistan tea-drinking is taken very seriously – black tea is served, with or without sugar. When tea is served, the more sugar added by the hostess, the more honored the guest.

# Ingredients

**Almonds**

Blanched almonds contribute crunch and subtle sweetness to pilafs, pastries and puddings. Ground almonds are used to thicken and flavor sauces.

**Pine nuts**

These ivory colored nuts are used in pilafs and stuffings.

**Pistachio nuts**

Their delicate flavor and color make them a favorite garnish for pastries, puddings and pilafs.

**Bulgur (Burghul)**

Hulled wheat, steamed dried and crushed. Available in fine, medium and coarse grinds, it requires soaking before use.

**Cardamom**

A spice that adds spicy sweetness to savory and sweet dishes.

**Chickpeas**

Dried legumes used in stews and soups, and for making falafel and hummus.

**Cilantro**

Feathery green leaves with a pungent flavor that enhances foods such as falafel.

**Cinnamon**

Bark from the cinnamon tree, dried and curled to form sticks.

**Almonds, pine nuts and pistachio nuts**

**Bulgur (Burghul)**

**Cardamom pods**

**Chickpeas (Garbanzo beans)**

**Cilantro (fresh coriander)**

**Cinnamon**

**Coriander and cumin**

**Cucumbers**

**Feta cheese**

**Flat-leaf parsley (Italian parsley)**

**Garlic chives**

**Haloumy cheese**

### Coriander
The seeds are dried and ground into a spice, with a combined flavor of lemon zest and sage.

### Cumin
Seeds with an aromatic earthy flavor that enhances other spices, such as coriander seeds.

### Cucumbers
The preferred cucumber to use in Middle Eastern dishes is the small, tender-skinned Lebanese cucumber, the English (hothouse) cucumber is the best substitute.

### Feta cheese
A Greek cheese traditionally produced from sheep's milk with a sharp, tangy flavor.

### Flat-leaf parsley
Common parsley of the region, also known as Italian parsley.

### Garlic chives
Flat-bladed chives with a garlic flavor. Substitute ordinary chives.

### Haloumy cheese
A salty sheep's milk cheese matured in brined whey. Haloumy is enjoyed as an eating cheese and is also panfried or grilled and served with a squeeze of lemon.

## Brown lentils and red lentils

Brown and green lentils are unhusked. The spicy-flavored, tiny red lentils are husked.

## Dried limes

Also known as black limes. Sun-dried limes are used to add a pleasant tartness to stews and soups. Lemon zest may be substituted.

## Mint

Spearmint is the preferred mint of the Middle East. If it is unavailable, dried mint may be substituted.

## Scallions

Also known as green onions. Always include 3–4 inches (8–10 cm) of the green tops.

## Olive oil

The most popular oil in the Mediterranean countries of the region. Use extra-virgin olive oil for dressing salads and vegetables, and pure olive oil for cooking.

## Orange flower water and rosewater

Fragrant, clear liquids distilled from orange blossoms and rose petals respectively. Used to perfume syrups, pastries and puddings.

## Orzo

A rice-shaped pasta also known as risoni.

**Lentils (brown and red)**

**Dried limes**

**Mint and scallions**

**Olive oil**

**Orange flower water and rosewater**

**Orzo**

**Pomegranates**

**Rice (long grain)**

**Rice (medium grain)**

**Saffron**

**Spinach**

**Tahini**

### Pomegranate

A fruit prized since ancient times for its sweet-tart juice and for its jewel-like seeds. The juice is made into a syrup. The seeds are sprinkled on savory dishes and puddings.

### Long-grain rice

White rice used for pilafs. Aromatic, cream-white basmati rice is preferred for some pilafs.

### Medium-grain rice

White rice used in stuffings for vegetables and grapevine leaves and for rice puddings.

### Saffron

The stigmas of *Crocus sativus*, picked by hand and dried in a labor-intensive process, making the final product the most expensive spice. Possessing a pungent, aromatic flavor and intense color, saffron is available as stigmas, or threads, and ground.

### Spinach

Native to Ancient Persia (Iran), spinach is a popular vegetable throughout the region, used in savory pastries and with beans, yogurt or eggs. The leaves can be curly or flat, depending on the season.

### Tahini

A smooth, oily paste made from ground toasted sesame seeds. For the best flavor, select a light-colored tahini.

1

2

3

4

# Step-by-Step
# Grapevine **leaves**

Select fresh leaves that are medium-light in color and not too young. The stems should be left attached as this prevents the leaves from tearing while blanching. Preserved leaves are available from Middle Eastern and Greek markets in jars, vacuum-packed in pouches, or in bulk; do not used canned leaves.

**1.** Rinse fresh leaves well; rinse brine from preserved leaves.

**2.** Bring a large saucepan of water to a boil, add a handful of fresh or preserved leaves and return to a boil. Boil for 1 minute, then transfer to a bowl of cold water with a slotted spoon. Let cool, then drain in a colander. Repeat with remaining leaves.

**3.** Snip the stem from each leaf with kitchen scissors. Place the leaf, shiny side down, on a work surface.

**4.** Place about 1 tablespoon filling at the stem end, just above the division at its base.

**5.** Fold each side of the leaf base diagonally over the filling so they overlap.

**6.** Roll the leaf once, fold the sides over the filling and then roll firmly to the end of leaf.

**7.** Line the bottom of a saucepan with damaged and/or extra leaves and pack the rolls in the saucepan, seam-side down, placing them close together.

**8.** Invert a heavy plate directly on top of the rolls, add liquid as specified in recipe (see page 30) and cook as directed.

**Other uses:**

Wrap fresh sardines or smelts in the leaves, brush with a mixture of olive oil and lemon juice and grill (barbecue) in a double-hinged wire basket. Larger fish that are cooked whole may be wrapped and grilled (barbecued) or baked in an oven. Quail and other small game birds may also be wrapped in vine leaves before roasting.

5

6

7

8

# Step-by-Step
# Handling **phyllo**

Phyllo, a Greek word meaning 'leaf,' is a delicate, tissue-thin pastry. It is available commercially either fresh (chilled) or frozen. If properly sealed, fresh phyllo can be stored in the refrigerator for several weeks, but must never be frozen. Frozen phyllo is more readily available at supermarkets. It varies slightly from fresh phyllo, a different formula being used to withstand the rigors of freezing.

Defrost frozen phyllo according to package directions. Leave defrosted or fresh phyllo at room temperature in its package for 2 hours before opening, otherwise sheets could break apart when opened out.

Remove phyllo from package and open out on a dry kitchen towel on a work surface. Cover phyllo with a dry, folded kitchen towel or a sheet of heavy-duty plastic wrap. A damp kitchen towel can be placed on top of the dry towel as insurance against the phyllo sheets drying. Phyllo dries out very quickly in the heat of the kitchen, so covering is essential, particularly if the shaping of individual pastries takes time. After using phyllo, fold any leftover sheets and return to plastic pouch, seal, replace in package and store in refrigerator. Do not refreeze frozen phyllo after it has been defrosted.

# Buttering phyllo

Work phyllo in a stack rather than buttering one sheet at a time. The process is quicker and there is less chance the sheets will dry and become brittle.

**1.** Take the number of sheets required and place on a work surface in a stack. Brush the top sheet with warm, melted unsalted or clarified butter or ghee. Olive oil may be used for savory dishes.

**2.** Lift a sheet, holding it at the corners nearest you, and turn it upside-down onto the stack. Flatten with your hand – it does not matter if phyllo wrinkles. Brush the top with butter or ghee, lift the top two brushed sheets and turn them upside-down onto the stack. Repeat, lifting an extra sheet each time, until all sheets in a stack are brushed. Leave the top and bottom sheets unbrushed. Use as required.

**3.** An alternative method is to fold the stack of phyllo sheets to resemble a book. Place on a work surface and turn the first "page" onto the work surface. Brush with butter or ghee, then turn and brush each "page." When the center is reached, leave unbrushed, fold the stack again, and butter the other side in the same manner.

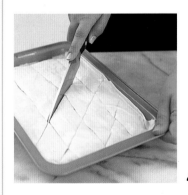

# Cutting diamond shapes

**4.** Brush the top and cut or score evenly placed lines along the length of the dish. The closer the lines, the smaller the final pieces will be – space the lines about $1^1/4$ inches (3 cm) apart for sweet dishes such as baklava, and wider apart for savory pies. Cut or score diagonally across the dish, spacing the lines evenly as for the first cuts. (Baked Kibbe, page 80, and Basbousa, page 116, may also be cut into diamonds in this way.)

# Step-by-Step
# Baked pastry **rolls**
## Burma börek

## Ingredients

SPINACH FILLING

1 tablespoon olive oil

1 medium yellow (brown) onion, finely chopped

1 cup (6 oz/185 g) well-drained, fresh or frozen spinach

²/₃ cup (4 oz/125 g) crumbled feta cheese

½ cup (4 oz/125 g) ricotta cheese

1 egg

3 tablespoons finely chopped fresh flat-leaf (Italian) parsley

1 tablespoon chopped fresh dill

salt

freshly ground black pepper

**1.** To make spinach filling, heat olive oil in a frying pan over medium–low heat. Add onion and fry until translucent, about 7 minutes. Finely chop spinach, place in a bowl and add onion and remaining filling ingredients, including salt and pepper to taste. If using cheese filling, mix all ingredients together in a bowl.

**2.** Preheat oven to 350°F (180°C/gas 4). Cut phyllo sheets in half crosswise to make squares approximately 10 inches (25 cm) in size. Stack and cover with a folded kitchen towel or a sheet of heavy-duty plastic wrap.

**3.** Put a sheet of phyllo on a work surface and brush half its width with butter. Fold in half and lightly brush the top with butter.

**CHEESE FILLING**

2 cups (10 oz/300 g) crumbled feta cheese

1 cup (8 oz/250 g) ricotta cheese

2 eggs

6 tablespoons finely chopped fresh flat-leaf (Italian) parsley

freshly ground black pepper

**FOR ROLLS**

18–20 sheets phyllo

½ cup (4 fl oz/125 ml) melted, unsalted butter

**4**

4. Place about 1 tablespoon of chosen filling in a thick strip along the narrow edge, about ³/₄ inch (2 cm) in from edge and sides of pastry.

5. Fold the phyllo over filling, fold in sides and roll firmly to the end of the sheet.

**5**

6. Place seam-side down on a lightly greased baking sheet. Repeat with remaining ingredients.

7. Lightly brush the tops of the rolls with melted butter. Bake until puffed and golden, about 20 minutes. Serve hot.

**Makes 36–40 rolls**
**Cooking time 20 minutes**

**6**

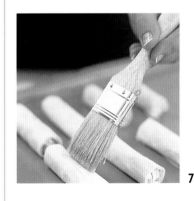

**7**

1

2

# Step-by-Step
# Drained yogurt

Yogurt required for Middle Eastern cooking should be the thick, plain (natural) variety made with whole (full-fat) milk. Greek-style yogurt is ideal. Low-fat yogurt is not used traditionally, although it may be used for dietary reasons. To check if yogurt is thick enough, make a hollow in yogurt with a spoon and leave in the refrigerator for 1 hour or more. If liquid appears in the hollow, then yogurt should be drained for recipes as indicated.

**1.** Line a large stainless steel or plastic strainer or colander with a double layer of moistened cheesecloth (muslin) and place over a bowl.

**2.** Spoon in the yogurt, cover with a plate and place in refrigerator for 2–4 hours, depending on type of yogurt used.

1

2

# Step-by-Step
# Yogurt cheese
## Labni (Lebanon, Syria)

**1.** In a bowl, stir 1$\frac{1}{2}$ teaspoons salt into 4 cups (2 lb/1 kg) plain whole-milk yogurt. Drain the yogurt for at least 12 hours following the above directions. The resulting consistency should be that of softened cream cheese.

**2.** Turn the yogurt into a bowl and chill in the refrigerator. Spread in a shallow dish, drizzle with a little olive oil, dust with paprika if desired and serve with pita bread.

# Step-by-Step
# Cooked yogurt
## Laban matboukh (Lebanon, Syria)

Yogurt must be stabilized to prevent it from curdling during cooking. Low-fat yogurt prepared in this way is an excellent substitute for sour cream or coconut milk used in other cuisines.

**1.** Place 2 cups (1 lb/500 g) plain whole-milk yogurt or low-fat yogurt in a heavy-bottomed saucepan.

**2.** In a small bowl, beat 1 egg white with a fork until frothy. Mix into yogurt with 2 teaspoons cornstarch (cornflour) and 1 teaspoon salt.

**3.** Bring the yogurt slowly to a boil over medium–low heat, stirring continuously with a wooden spoon. Reduce heat to low and simmer gently until thick, 3–5 minutes. Use as directed in individual recipes, but do not cover food being cooked in the stabilized yogurt as the moisture from the lid will destabilize the yogurt.

## Ingredients

2 cloves garlic

½ teaspoon salt, plus extra salt to taste

¾ cup (6 fl oz/185 ml) tahini

⅓ cup (3 fl oz/90 ml) cold water

⅓ cup (3 fl oz/90 ml) lemon juice

**Note:** In Cyprus this sauce is known as tahinosalata.

# Tahini sauce
## Taratour bi tahine
### (Lebanon, Syria, Jordan)

In a small bowl, crush garlic with ½ teaspoon salt and mix to a paste. Gradually add tahini, beating well with a wooden spoon.

Then alternately beat in small amounts of water and lemon juice. The water will thicken the mixture; lemon juice will thin it. Add all the lemon juice, and enough water to give the sauce a thin or thick consistency, depending on use. The flavor should be tart. Add salt to taste if necessary. Use the sauce as a dip with pita bread or as an accompaniment for falafel, fried or poached fish, or boiled cauliflower or potatoes.

**Food processor method:** Place tahini and garlic in processor bowl and process for a few seconds to crush garlic. Add lemon juice and water alternately, a small amount at a time, until desired consistency is reached. Blend in salt to taste.

**Makes 1½ cups (12 fl oz/375 ml)**

## Variation

### Parsley and tahini sauce (Bakdounis bi tahini)

Follow directions for Tahini sauce, adding 3–4 tablespoons finely chopped flat-leaf (Italian) parsley after blending half the water and all the lemon juice into the tahini. Beat well and add more water if necessary. If using a food processor, add parsley after all other ingredients are blended and process for a few seconds. Serve as a dip, or as an accompaniment to simple fish dishes.

**Makes 1½ cups (12 fl oz/375 ml)**

# Chickpea **patties**

## Falafel (Lebanon, Syria)

Put chickpeas in a bowl, add water and soak in a cool place for 12–15 hours or overnight.

Drain chickpeas and rinse well. (Do not cook chickpeas as patties would disintegrate when fried).

In a bowl, combine soaked chickpeas with onion, garlic, parsley, cilantro, ground chili, coriander, cumin, baking soda, salt and pepper. Toss ingredients lightly to mix.

Process mixture in batches in a food processor until finely ground. Alternatively, the mixture can be passed through a food grinder twice, using a fine screen.

Place the ground mixture in a bowl and knead well so that it just holds together. Cover and set aside for 30 minutes.

With moistened hands, shape generous tablespoonfuls of mixture into balls, then flatten into thick patties 1½ inches (4 cm) in diameter. Place on a baking sheet and set aside for 15 minutes.

Pour oil into a heavy frying pan over medium heat, to a depth of 1 inch (2.5 cm). When the oil reaches 375°F (190°C) on a deep-frying thermometer, add 6–8 patties at a time and cook, turning once, until deep golden brown, 3–4 minutes. Remove with a slotted spoon and drain on paper towels.

Serve hot as an appetizer with Tahini Sauce or in pita bread with the sauce and salad ingredients, including Tabbouleh.

**Makes about 30 patties**
**Cooking time 3–4 minutes per batch**

**Note:** Do not use a large onion as this will make the mixture too soft.

## Ingredients

1½ cups (10 oz/300 g) dried chickpeas (garbanzo beans)

4 cups (32 fl oz/1 L) cold water

1 medium yellow (brown) onion, coarsely chopped

2 cloves garlic

6 tablespoons chopped fresh flat-leaf (Italian) parsley

3 tablespoons chopped fresh cilantro (fresh coriander)

pinch ground red chili

1 teaspoon ground coriander

½ teaspoon ground cumin

½ teaspoon baking soda (bicarbonate of soda)

1 teaspoon salt

freshly ground pepper to taste

vegetable oil for deep-frying

Tahini Sauce (page 26) for serving

Tabbouleh (page 43) for serving

## Ingredients

1 cup (6 oz/180 g) dried chickpeas (garbanzo beans)

3 cups (24 fl oz/750 ml) water

1½ teaspoons salt, plus extra salt to taste

⅓ cup (3 fl oz/85 ml) tahini

½ cup (4 fl oz/125 ml) lemon juice

2 cloves garlic, crushed

FOR GARNISH

1 tablespoon olive oil

chopped fresh parsley

paprika or cayenne pepper

# Chickpea and **sesame** puree

## Hummus bi tahini

### (Lebanon, Syria, Jordan)

Put chickpeas in a bowl, add water and soak in a cool place for 12 hours or overnight. Drain and rinse well.

Place chickpeas in a saucepan with fresh water to cover. Bring to boil, cover and cook over low heat for 1 hour. Add 1 teaspoon salt and cook until very tender, about 30 minutes longer. Drain, and reserve some cooking liquid and 1 tablespoon chickpeas.

Press chickpeas through a sieve or food mill into a bowl, adding about 2 tablespoons cooking liquid to separate the last of the peas from their skins.

Slowly blend tahini and most of the lemon juice into chickpea puree.

In a bowl, crush garlic with ½ teaspoon salt and mix to a paste. Add to puree. Adjust flavor and consistency with remaining lemon juice or cooking liquid, and add salt if necessary. Hummus should be thick and smooth.

Spread puree in a shallow serving dish, swirling with back of a spoon. Drizzle olive oil in center and garnish with reserved chickpeas, chopped parsley and a sprinkling of paprika or cayenne.

**Food processor method:** Place cooked chickpeas in processor bowl with remaining ingredients, reserving some lemon juice and salt. Process until thick and smooth, adding cooking liquid, lemon juice and salt to adjust consistency and flavor. The hummus will not be as smooth as when made with the sieved method, but is quicker to prepare.

**Makes 3 cups (24 fl oz/750 ml)**
**Cooking time 1½ hours**

# Meatball soup

## Yourvarlakia avgolemono

### (Cyprus)

In a bowl, mix lamb with onion, egg, rice, parsley, mint (if using), and salt and pepper to taste. Shape into meatballs the size of a small walnut and coat lightly with flour.

Bring stock to a boil in a soup pot, season with salt and pepper if necessary and drop in meatballs. Add butter. Cover and simmer for 1 hour.

In a bowl, beat eggs until light and foamy. Gradually beat in lemon juice. Slowly add about 2 cups (16 fl oz/500 ml) simmering stock, beating constantly.

Pour egg mixture into soup and stir constantly over low heat for 2 minutes to cook egg, then remove from heat and stir for 1 minute longer so the heat of the pot will not cause the egg to curdle.

Ladle soup into deep soup bowls and sprinkle with chopped parsley. Serve with bread.

**Serves 6**
**Cooking time 1 hour**

## Ingredients

1 lb (500 g) finely ground (minced) lamb

1 small yellow (brown) onion, finely chopped

1 egg, beaten

1/3 cup (2½ oz/75 g) medium-grain rice

2 tablespoons finely chopped fresh flat-leaf (Italian) parsley

1 teaspoon finely chopped fresh mint, optional

salt

freshly ground black pepper

all-purpose (plain) flour for coating

5 cups (40 fl oz/1.25 L) lamb or chicken stock

1 tablespoon butter

2 eggs

juice of 1 lemon

chopped fresh flat-leaf (Italian) parsley for garnish

crusty bread for serving

## Ingredients

1½ cups (10 oz/300 g) dried brown lentils

6 cups (48 fl oz/1.5L) cold water

8–10 Swiss chard (silverbeet) leaves

¼ cup (2 fl oz/60 ml) olive oil

1 large yellow (brown) onion, finely chopped

3 cloves garlic, finely chopped

3 tablespoons chopped fresh cilantro (fresh coriander)

salt

freshly ground black pepper

¼ cup (2 fl oz/60 ml) lemon juice

extra-virgin olive oil

lemon wedges

pita or other bread

# Lentil and Swiss **chard** soup

## Adas bis silq (Lebanon, Syria, Jordan)

Rinse lentils well in a sieve under cold running water. Place in a heavy saucepan with cold water. Bring to a boil, skimming surface if necessary, then cover and simmer until lentils are tender, 25–30 minutes.

Wash chard well and cut off stems, reserving them for another use. Slit leaves down the middle, then shred coarsely.

In another heavy saucepan over medium–low heat, warm olive oil. Add onion and gently fry until translucent. Stir in garlic and cook for a few seconds longer.

Add shredded chard to pan and fry, stirring often, until leaves wilt.

Add onion and chard to lentils, along with cilantro, salt and pepper to taste, and lemon juice. Cover and simmer for 10 minutes longer. Serve soup in deep soup bowls with olive oil and lemon wedges for squeezing. Pita or other bread is a necessary accompaniment.

**Serves 5–6**
**Cooking time 35–40 minutes**

## Ingredients

1½ cups (10 oz/300 g) dried red lentils

6 cups (48 fl oz/1.5 L) meat or chicken stock or water

1 yellow (brown) onion, grated

1 teaspoon ground cumin

salt

freshly ground black pepper

1 tablespoon lemon juice

FOR TA'LEYA

2 large yellow (brown) onions

¼ cup (2 fl oz/60 ml) olive oil

1–2 cloves garlic, finely chopped

olive oil for serving

lemon wedges for serving

# Red lentil soup

## Shourba ads (Egypt)

Rinse lentils well in a sieve under cold running water.

Bring stock or water to a boil in a large soup pot. Add lentils and onion. Reduce heat to low, cover and simmer until lentils are tender, about 30 minutes. Do not stir during cooking. The lentils should have collapsed into a puree; for a finer texture, pass through a sieve or puree in a blender.

Add cumin and salt and pepper to taste. If a thinner soup is desired, add water. Stir in lemon juice and heat gently.

To prepare Ta'leya, cut each onion in half lengthwise and thinly slice each half crosswise into semicircles. Heat ¼ cup (2 fl oz/60 ml) oil in a frying pan over medium heat. Add onions and cook, stirring often, until golden brown, about 10 minutes. Add garlic, cook for a few seconds and remove from heat.

Serve the hot soup in deep soup bowls, topping each serving with Ta'leya. Offer extra olive oil to drizzle, and provide lemon wedges for squeezing into the soup.

**Serves 6**
**Cooking time 45 minutes**

# Cold yogurt soup

## Mast va khiar (Iran)

Peel cucumbers if necessary and coarsely grate into a bowl. Add yogurt and raisins.

Finely slice scallions and add to yogurt with parsley and dill, walnuts (if using) and eggs. Season with salt.

Stir in sufficient ice water for a creamy consistency and adjust flavor with salt if necessary. Cover and chill for at least 2 hours.

Serve in soup bowls garnished with chopped herbs or herb sprigs.

**Serves 6**

**Note:** Low-fat yogurt may be used; add an extra cup (8 oz/250 g) and omit ice water.

## Ingredients

2 young green cucumbers or ½ English (hothouse) cucumber

3 cups (24 oz/750 g) plain whole-milk yogurt

½ cup (3 oz/90 g) golden raisins (sultanas)

3 scallions (shallots/spring onions) including tender green tops

1 tablespoon finely chopped fresh flat-leaf (Italian) parsley

1 tablespoon finely chopped fresh dill

½ cup (2 oz/60 g) finely chopped walnuts, optional

2 hard-cooked eggs, finely chopped

salt

about 1 cup (8 fl oz/250 ml) ice water

parsley and/or dill for garnish

# Bulgur and **parsley** salad

## Tabbouleh (Lebanon, Syria, Jordan)

### Ingredients

- ³/₄ cup (4 oz/125 g) fine bulgur (burghul)
- 2 cups (16 fl oz/500 ml) cold water
- 5 scallions (shallots/spring onions), finely chopped, including tender green tops
- 4 cups (6 oz/180 g) coarsely chopped fresh flat-leaf (Italian) parsley
- 3 tablespoons finely chopped fresh mint
- ¼ cup (2 fl oz/60 ml) olive oil
- 2 tablespoons lemon juice
- 1½ teaspoons salt
- ½ teaspoon freshly ground black pepper
- 2 firm, ripe tomatoes
- crisp romaine (cos) lettuce leaves
- ¼ cup (2 fl oz/60 ml) lemon juice mixed with 1/2 teaspoon salt

Place bulgur in a bowl and cover with cold water. Let soak for 15 minutes. Drain through a fine-mesh sieve, pressing with back of a spoon to extract moisture. Spread onto a kitchen towel to dry further.

Put bulgur in a bowl and add scallions. Squeeze mixture with hands so bulgur absorbs onion flavor.

Add parsley and mint to bulgur.

In a small bowl, beat olive oil with lemon juice. Stir in salt and pepper. Add to salad and toss well.

Peel tomatoes as follows: place in a bowl, pour boiling water over, and let stand for 10 seconds. Drain, peel, remove seeds, then dice. Gently stir tomatoes into salad. Cover and chill for at least 1 hour before serving.

Serve in a shallow salad bowl lined with lettuce leaves. Serve the lemon juice and salt mixture alongside, so it can be added according to individual taste.

**Serves 6–8**

# Village salad
## Salata horiatiko (Cyprus)

### Ingredients

8 romaine (cos) lettuce leaves

small bunch arugula (rocket)

4 medium tomatoes

2 young green cucumbers or
½ English (hothouse) cucumber

1 green bell pepper (capsicum),
halved, cored and seeded

2 medium red onions, sliced

4 oz (125 g) feta cheese, diced

½ cup (3 oz/90 g) black olives

DRESSING

⅓ cup (3 fl oz/90 ml) extra-virgin
olive oil

1 tablespoon white wine vinegar

2 teaspoons finely chopped fresh
flat-leaf (Italian) parsley

1 teaspoon finely chopped fresh mint

salt

freshly ground black pepper

Wash lettuce and arugula, and dry. Tear lettuce into large pieces and arugula into small pieces.

If peeled tomatoes are desired, place in a bowl, pour boiling water over, and let stand for 10 seconds. Drain and peel. Cut into wedges.

Peel cucumber and halve lengthwise. Cut crosswise into ½-inch (1-cm) slices. Cut bell pepper into thick strips. Separate onion slices into rings.

To make dressing, combine oil, vinegar, parsley and mint in a small bowl. Whisk together, then add salt and pepper to taste.

Place lettuce, arugula, tomatoes, cucumbers, bell peppers and onions in a bowl. Top with feta cheese and olives. Pour on dressing just before serving and toss.

Serves 6

# Tomato salad
## Banadura salata bil kizbara
### (Yemen)

### Ingredients

6 medium-sized, firm tomatoes,
peeled

6 tablespoons chopped fresh cilantro
(fresh coriander)

1 small hot chili pepper, or freshly
ground black pepper

juice of ½ lemon

about 1 teaspoon salt

¼ cup (2 fl oz/60 ml) olive oil

Slice tomatoes into a bowl and sprinkle layers with cilantro.

If using chili, cut off stem, slit open and remove seeds. Take care that you do not touch your face. Finely chop the chili.

In a small bowl, combine chopped chili or ground pepper with lemon juice and salt. Beat in olive oil. Pour over tomatoes and let stand for 15 minutes before serving.

Serves 6

# Toasted bread salad

## Fattoush (Lebanon, Syria, Jordan)

Toast pita bread until golden brown. Break into small pieces or cut into small squares using kitchen scissors.

Shred lettuce or break into small pieces. Peel cucumber if desired, quarter lengthwise and cut into chunks. Cut tomatoes into small cubes.

To make dressing, crush garlic in a small bowl with salt and mix to a paste. Add lemon juice, olive oil and pepper, then beat thoroughly with a fork.

In a salad bowl, combine bread, lettuce, cucumber, tomatoes, bell pepper, scallions, parsley and mint. Pour on dressing, toss well and serve.

**Serves 6**

## Ingredients

1 large pita bread

8 romaine (cos) lettuce leaves, or 6 leaves of another variety

1 young green cucumber or ¼ English (hothouse) cucumber

2 medium tomatoes

1 cup (5 oz/150 g) chopped green bell pepper (capsicum)

5 scallions (shallots/spring onions), chopped, including tender green tops

6 tablespoons chopped fresh flat-leaf (Italian) parsley

3 tablespoons chopped fresh mint

DRESSING

1 clove garlic

1 teaspoon salt

½ cup (4 fl oz/125 ml) lemon juice

½ cup (4 fl oz/125 ml) olive oil

freshly ground black pepper

## Ingredients

6 medium beets (beetroots) with tops

salt

DRESSING (OPTIONAL)

⅓ cup (3 fl oz/90 ml) extra-virgin olive oil

2 tablespoons red wine vinegar

1 tablespoon finely chopped fresh cilantro (fresh coriander), optional

## Ingredients

4–5 cloves garlic, halved

¼ cup (2 fl oz/60 ml) white wine vinegar

½ teaspoon salt, plus extra salt to taste

4 oz (125 g) stale, crustless, white Italian bread

½ cup ground blanched almonds

½ cup (4 fl oz/125 ml) olive oil, or as needed

1 tablespoon lemon juice, or as needed

freshly ground white pepper

# Beet with **garlic** sauce
## Pantzaria salata (Cyprus)

Cut tops from beets, leaving about 1¼ inches (3 cm) intact. Reserve tender, undamaged greens; discard remainder. Place beets in a saucepan, add water to cover and season with salt.

Bring to a boil and cook beets until tender, 30–45 minutes. In another saucepan of salted water, cook greens for 10 minutes.

Peel beets and slice or cube into a bowl. Drain greens and add to bowl if desired or place in a separate bowl.

If using dressing, combine all dressing ingredients in a small bowl, pour over hot beets and greens, toss gently and allow to cool before serving. Alternatively, serve beets and greens with Garlic sauce (see below).

**Serves 6–8**
**Cooking time 30–45 minutes**

# Garlic **sauce**
## Skorthalia (Cyprus)

In a small bowl, combine garlic and vinegar. Let stand for 10 minutes. Remove garlic from vinegar, place in a mortar, add ½ teaspoon salt and pound to a paste with a pestle. Set vinegar aside.

Soak bread in cold water and squeeze dry. Crumble into small pieces and gradually blend into garlic, adding a small amount of reserved vinegar to make a smooth mixture.

Transfer bread mixture to a bowl. Gradually beat in almonds and olive oil alternately with remaining vinegar. Beat in lemon juice and add salt and white pepper to taste. If mixture is very thick, beat in slightly more oil or lemon juice, depending on flavor desired. Mixture should be the consistency of stiff mayonnaise.

Transfer to a serving bowl. Serve with fried fish, squid or fried or boiled vegetables, or as directed in individual recipes.

**Food processor method:** Let garlic stand in vinegar for 10 minutes. Place all ingredients except oil in processor bowl and process until smooth. Gradually add oil. Adjust seasoning, flavor and consistency as described above, and process sauce until smooth. Do not overprocess as mixture could heat and curdle.

**Makes 1¹/₂ cups (12 fl oz/375 ml)**

# White **bean** salad

## Piyaz (Turkey)

Place beans in a bowl, add cold water, and let soak in a cool place for 8–10 hours. Drain and rinse beans, and place in a saucepan with fresh water to cover.

Bring beans to a boil, cover and simmer over low heat until tender but still intact, 1¹/₂–2 hours. Add salt to taste after 1¹/₄ hours cooking. Drain the beans well and turn into a bowl.

In a small bowl, crush garlic with a small amount of salt and mix to a paste. Halve onions lengthwise then thinly slice crosswise into semicircles. Add to hot beans with lemon juice, vinegar and oils. Set aside to cool.

Gently mix in parsley, mint and dill. Cover salad and chill for 1–2 hours.

Serve salad in a deep bowl garnished with bell pepper and hard-cooked eggs.

**Serves 6–8**
**Cooking time 1¹/₂–2 hours**

## Ingredients

2 cups (14 oz/440 g) dried cannellini beans

6 cups (48 fl oz/1.5 L) cold water

salt

1 clove garlic

2 small yellow (brown) onions

¼ cup (2 fl oz/60 ml) lemon juice

1 tablespoon distilled white vinegar

¼ cup (2 fl oz/60 ml) olive oil

¼ cup (2 fl oz/60 ml) sunflower oil

3 tablespoons chopped fresh flat-leaf (Italian) parsley

1 teaspoon chopped fresh mint

2 teaspoons chopped fresh dill

FOR GARNISH

1 green bell pepper (capsicum), cored, seeded and sliced

3 hard-cooked eggs, sliced or quartered

SEAFOOD

# Braised **octopus** and onions

## Oktapothi stifatho (Cyprus)

Pull tentacles from octopus and set aside. Remove intestines, ink sac, eyes and beak and discard. Wash head and tentacles and pull skin from head.

Place head and tentacles in a saucepan, cover and cook over medium heat until octopus releases its juice, about 10 minutes. Drain, let cool, and cut into bite-sized pieces.

Heat oil in a heavy frying pan over medium heat, and gently fry chopped onion until translucent, about 7 minutes. Add garlic and octopus and fry for 5 minutes.

Add tomato puree, wine, vinegar, salt and pepper to taste, cloves and cinnamon stick. Cover and simmer over low heat for 30 minutes.

Peel boiling (pickling) onions and cut an X in the root end of each. Add to pan; cover and cook until octopus is tender, about 1 hour.

Remove cloves and cinnamon stick, adjust seasonings and serve octopus with a plain rice pilaf.

**Serves 6**
**Cooking time 2 hours**

### Ingredients

1 octopus, about 2 lb (1 kg)

¼ cup (2 fl oz/60 ml) corn oil

1 medium yellow (brown) onion, chopped

2 cloves garlic, finely chopped

1 cup (8 fl oz/250 ml) tomato puree

¼ cup (2 fl oz/60 ml) dry red wine

¼ cup (2 fl oz/60 ml) red wine vinegar

salt

freshly ground black pepper

2 whole cloves

1 cinnamon stick, about 3 inches (8 cm) long

1½ lb (750 g) small boiling (pickling) onions

# Baked **fish** with **hot** chili **sauce**

## Samke harrah (Lebanon, Syria, Jordan)

### Ingredients

- 1 snapper or other white-fleshed fish, about 4 lb (2 kg)
- 1 teaspoon salt, plus extra salt to taste
- 4 tablespoons olive oil
- 4–6 cloves garlic
- 3 tablespoons finely chopped fresh cilantro (fresh coriander)
- 1 cup (8 fl oz/250 ml) tahini
- ½ cup (4 fl oz/ 125 ml) cold water
- ½ cup (4 fl oz/ 125 ml) lemon juice
- ¼–½ teaspoon ground red chili
- 1 tablespoon pine nuts
- lemon wedges for garnish
- fresh cilantro (fresh coriander) sprigs for garnish

Clean fish and remove scales if necessary. Leave head on but remove eyes. Rinse fish and pat dry with paper towels. Cut two slashes on each side. Sprinkle fish inside and out with salt, place on a plate, cover and refrigerate for 1–2 hours. Pat dry again before cooking.

Heat 3 tablespoons oil in a large heavy frying pan over high heat. Add fish and cook for 3–4 minutes on each side. Do not cook through. Remove fish from pan and place in a baking dish (roasting pan).

In a mortar with pestle, pound garlic to a paste with 1 teaspoon salt and mix in cilantro. Remove some oil from the frying pan, leaving about 2 tablespoons. Heat remaining oil over medium heat and add garlic mixture. Fry until mixture is crisp. Return to mortar and let cool.

Preheat oven to 350°F (180°C/gas 4).

Place tahini in a bowl, beat well, then gradually add cold water, beating constantly. Mixture will thicken. Gradually beat in lemon juice, and stir in garlic mixture and ground chili to taste. Add more salt to taste if necessary.

Pour sauce over fish, covering it completely. Bake until fish is cooked through and sauce is bubbling, 30–35 minutes.

While fish cooks, heat remaining 1 tablespoon olive oil in a small frying pan over medium heat. Add pine nuts and toast, stirring constantly, until golden, 2–3 minutes. Remove immediately from pan to a plate to prevent burning.

Lift cooked fish onto a platter and spoon sauce on top. Sprinkle with pine nuts and garnish platter with lemon wedges and cilantro sprigs. Serve hot.

**Serves 4**
**Cooking time 40–45 minutes**

## Ingredients

1½ lb (750 g) fish steaks or fillets

salt

2 tablespoons ghee or oil

2 medium yellow (brown) onions, chopped

1 teaspoon peeled and grated fresh ginger

2 cloves garlic, crushed

½ teaspoon ground red chili

1 teaspoon baharat (page 120)

1 teaspoon turmeric

1 cinnamon stick, about 1½ inches (4 cm) long

1 cup (6 oz/180 g) chopped, peeled tomatoes

2 dried limes or zest of ½ lemon

½ cup (4 fl oz/125 ml) water

Rice with Onion (page 105) for serving

# Fish curry

## Samak quwarmah (Gulf States)

Rinse fish and pat dry with paper towels. Cut into serving sizes and sprinkle lightly with salt. Place on a plate, cover and set aside.

Heat ghee or oil in a heavy frying pan over medium–low heat. Add onion and cook until translucent, about 10 minutes. Add ginger, garlic, chili, Baharat, turmeric and cinnamon stick and cook, stirring, for 2 minutes.

Add tomatoes, dried limes (pierced twice with a skewer) or lemon zest, and water. Add salt to taste, cover and simmer for 15 minutes.

Place fish pieces in sauce, cover and simmer until fish is cooked through, 15–20 minutes. Lift fish onto a platter with prepared Rice with Onion. Remove dried lime or lemon zest and cinnamon stick from sauce and spoon sauce over fish. Serve hot.

**Serves 6**
**Cooking time 45–50 minutes**

## Ingredients

2 cups (14 oz/220 g) long-grain rice

3 lb (1.5 kg) small mussels

½ cup (4 fl oz/125 ml) olive oil

1 large yellow (brown) onion, finely chopped

fish stock or bottled clam juice

1 tablespoon lemon juice

salt

freshly ground black pepper

3 tablespoons chopped fresh flat-leaf (Italian) parsley

1 tablespoon chopped fresh dill

herb sprigs and lemon wedges for garnish

# Mussel pilaf
## Midyeli pilav (Turkey)

Place rice in a fine-mesh sieve and rinse under cold running water until water runs clear. Drain well.

Tap any open mussels and discard if they do not close. Put into cold water and move them about gently. Take out one at a time and tug the beard toward the pointed end to remove. Place in a bowl of clean water once debearded.

Drain mussels, put in a large pot, cover and cook on high heat, shaking the pot occasionally just long enough to open mussles, about 5 minutes. Place opened mussels in a bowl and cover to keep warm; return any unopened mussels to the pot and heat a little longer. If they do not open, discard. Strain mussel juices through a fine-mesh sieve into a bowl, and set aside.

Heat oil in a deep saucepan over medium–low heat. Add onion and cook until translucent, about 8 minutes. Add drained rice and stir over medium heat for 2 minutes.

Measure mussel liquor and add stock or clam juice to make 3½ cups (22 fl oz/825 ml). Add to rice with lemon juice, 1½ teaspoons salt and pepper to taste, and stir in parsley and dill. Bring to a boil, stirring occasionally. Reduce heat, cover pan tightly and cook over low heat for 18 minutes.

While rice is cooking, remove all but six mussels from shells.

Put shelled mussels on top of rice. Place two paper towels over rim of pan and fit lid on firmly. Cook over low heat for 3 minutes longer, then remove from heat and let stand for 5 minutes.

Gently stir mussels through rice with a fork. Transfer pilaf to a serving dish. Garnish with reserved 6 mussels with shells, herb sprigs and lemon wedges, and serve hot.

**Serves 6**
**Cooking time 40 minutes**

# Spiced **shrimp** and rice

## Machbous (Gulf States)

In a large pot over high heat, heat 1 tablespoon ghee. Add garlic and shrimp and cook, stirring frequently, until shrimp turn pink. Remove shrimp to a plate and set aside.

Add remaining ghee to the pot and heat over medium–low heat. Add onion and cook until translucent and lightly browned, about 8 minutes. Stir in Baharat and turmeric and cook for 1 minute.

Add tomatoes, salt, pepper to taste, parsley and cilantro. Bring to a boil and add water. Cover and cook over medium heat for 5 minutes.

Place rice in a fine-mesh sieve and rinse under cold running water until water runs clear. Stir into sauce and bring to a boil. Reduce heat to low, cover and cook for 18 minutes.

Stir rice, then put shrimp on top of rice and gently stir through rice. Cover pot and simmer over low heat for 3 minutes.

Stir rice again then leave covered, off the heat, for 5 minutes. Serve with pita bread, pickles and salad.

**Serves 4–5**
**Cooking time 40 minutes**

## Ingredients

2–3 tablespoons ghee or vegetable oil

2 cloves garlic, chopped

2 lb (1 kg) raw shrimp (prawns), shelled and deveined

1 large yellow (brown) onion, chopped

2 teaspoons baharat (page 120)

2 teaspoons turmeric

1½ cups (9 oz/280 g) chopped, peeled tomatoes

2 teaspoons salt

freshly ground black pepper

1 tablespoon chopped fresh flat-leaf (Italian) parsley

1 teaspoon chopped fresh cilantro (fresh coriander)

2½ cups (20 fl oz/625 ml) water

2 cups (14 oz/440 g) basmati rice

CHICKEN

# Circassian chicken

## Çerkes tavugu (Turkey)

Place chicken in a saucepan with onion, carrot, parsley and cold water. Bring to a slow simmer, skimming surface as needed. Add salt and pepper to taste. Cover and simmer until thigh joint moves freely when leg is pushed, about 1½ hours; do not boil as this makes meat stringy. Remove pan from heat and let cool slightly. Transfer chicken to a plate. Strip off meat and return skin and bones to pan. Boil stock with bones and skin until reduced by half. Strain and reserve chicken stock, skimming off fat from surface.

Cut meat into 2-inch (5-cm) strips and place in a bowl. Moisten with 2 tablespoons chicken stock, cover and refrigerate.

Soak bread in a small amount of stock, squeeze out excess moisture and crumble into a food processor bowl. Add walnuts, paprika and garlic, if using, and pulse to combine. With motor running, slowly add 1 cup (8 fl oz/250 ml) warm chicken stock, adding slightly more if necessary to make a smooth, thick sauce. Adjust seasoning with salt and pepper.

Gently mix one-third of walnut sauce into chilled chicken. Shape chicken into an attractive mound on a shallow dish and spread remaining sauce on top. Cover lightly with plastic wrap and refrigerate.

To prepare garnish, steep paprika in walnut oil for at least 10 minutes in a small bowl. Drizzle over the top of the chicken just before serving. Garnish with parsley if desired. Serve cold.

**Serves 6**
**Cooking time 1½ hours**

## Ingredients

1 chicken, about 3 lb (1.5 kg)

1 large yellow (brown) onion, quartered

1 carrot, quartered

2 sprigs fresh flat-leaf (Italian) parsley or curly-leaf parsley

3 cups (24 fl oz/750 ml) cold water

1½ teaspoons salt

freshly ground white pepper

3 slices stale white Italian bread, crusts removed

1½ cups (6 oz/180 g) finely ground walnuts

½ teaspoon paprika

1 clove garlic, crushed, optional

FOR GARNISH

½ teaspoon paprika

1 tablespoon walnut oil

finely chopped parsley, optional

## Ingredients

RICE STUFFING

½ cup (3½ oz/105 g) basmati rice

¼ cup (2 oz/60 g) butter or ghee

1 small yellow (brown) onion, finely chopped

¼ cup (1½ oz/45 g) pine nuts or slivered blanched almonds

¼ cup (1 oz/30 g) chopped walnuts

¼ cup (1½ oz/45 g) golden raisins (sultanas)

½ teaspoon baharat (page 120) or ground allspice

1 cup (8 fl oz/250 ml) water

salt

freshly ground black pepper

1 chicken, about 3½ lb (1.75 kg)

¼ cup (2 fl oz/60 ml) melted butter or ghee

½ cup (4 fl oz/125 ml) water or chicken stock

# Roast **stuffed** chicken
## Dijaj ala timman (Iraq)

Place rice in a fine-mesh sieve and rinse under cold running water until water runs clear. Drain well.

Melt butter or ghee in a saucepan over medium–high heat. Add onion and fry gently until translucent, about 7 minutes. Stir in pine nuts or almonds, walnuts and rice, and fry, stirring often, for 5 minutes.

Add raisins, Baharat, water and salt and pepper to taste. Stir well, cover and cook over low heat until water is absorbed, about 10 minutes. Remove from heat and let cool.

Preheat oven to 350°F (180°C/gas 4). Rinse chicken and pat dry with paper towels. Fill cavity with rice stuffing, and truss. Rub chicken with salt and pepper.

Coat a baking dish (roasting pan) with some of the melted butter or ghee. Put chicken in pan and baste with remaining butter or ghee. Add water or stock to pan. Roast chicken, basting often with liquid, until juices run clear when pierced at the thigh, about 1½–2 hours.

Spoon stuffing into the center of a platter. Cut chicken into serving portions and arrange around stuffing.

**Serves 6**
**Cooking time 2 hours**

**Note:** Juices remaining in the baking dish (roasting pan) after the chicken is cooked may be skimmed, diluted with a little stock, brought to a boil and served in a pitcher, although this is not a customary accompaniment.

# Pot roasted chicken

## Tashreeb dijaj (Iraq)

Rinse chicken and pat dry with paper towels. Cut half of the lemon into quarters. Rub chicken inside and out with lemon pieces. Season cavity and skin of chicken with salt and pepper. Set aside on a plate for 30 minutes to allow chicken to absorb flavors.

Heat ghee or oil in a heavy saucepan or Dutch oven over medium–high heat. Add chicken and brown on all sides, turning as needed.

Remove outer papery layers from head of garlic, exposing cloves. Leave cloves unpeeled and attached to root. Rinse well and add to chicken. Reduce heat to low, cover and cook for 10 minutes.

Juice the remaining lemon half and add to chicken with water. Cover pan tightly and simmer over low heat until tender, turning chicken twice during cooking, about 1 1/2 hours.

Remove chicken to a platter and keep warm. Skim fat from juices in pan. Remove garlic and discard. Place pan over high heat and cook until liquid is reduced by half, about 10 minutes. Adjust seasoning with salt and pepper.

Cut chicken into serving portions and pour juices over chicken. Serve with Saffron Rice or Rice Pilaf.

**Serves 6**
**Cooking time 2 hours**

### Ingredients

1 chicken, about 3 1/2 lb (1.75 kg)

1 lemon

salt

freshly ground black pepper

2 tablespoons ghee or vegetable oil

1 head garlic, left whole and unpeeled

1 cup (8 fl oz/250 ml) water

Saffron Rice (page 104) for serving

Rice Pilaf (page 102) for serving

## Ingredients

2 chickens, each about 2 lb (1 kg)

½ cup (4 fl oz/125 ml) lemon juice

1 large yellow (brown) onion, grated

2 teaspoons salt

freshly ground black pepper

¼ cup (2 fl oz/60 ml) melted ghee or
butter

1 teaspoon paprika

Steamed Rice (page 103) for serving

cherry tomatoes for garnish

# Skewered grilled chicken

## Joojeh kabab (Iran)

Cut each chicken in half lengthwise and remove backbone. Cut each half into six pieces that are nearly equal in size: halve breast pieces and thighs, chop off bony end of leg, and leave each wing intact.

Combine lemon juice, onion, salt and pepper to taste in a glass or ceramic bowl. Add chicken pieces, turning in marinade to coat. Let marinate for 3–4 hours in refrigerator, turning chicken occasionally.

Prepare a fire in a grill (barbecue), preferably charcoal, or preheat a broiler (griller).

Thread chicken onto six long, flat metal skewers, placing the thicker pieces in the center, and packing all the pieces close together. In a small bowl, combine melted ghee or butter with paprika and brush over chicken. Place chicken on a grill (barbecue) rack or under the broiler (griller) and cook, basting frequently with ghee mixture and turning often, until chicken is cooked through, 15–20 minutes.

Remove chicken from skewers if desired and serve with Steamed Rice. Garnish with blistered cherry tomatoes.

**To blister cherry tomatoes:** Cut an X on the bottom of each tomato and thread onto skewers if necessary. Brush with melted butter or ghee and cook on a grill (barbecue) rack or under a broiler (griller) until skin blisters and browns lightly.

**Serves 6**
**Cooking time 15–20 minutes**

# Orange **rice** with **chicken**

## Zarda palau (Afghanistan)

Remove zest from oranges with vegetable peeler and cut into fine shreds about 1¹/₄ inches (3 cm) long. Bring water to a boil in a small saucepan. Add zest and boil for 5 minutes. Drain and rinse.

Place 1 cup (8 fl oz/250 ml) water in same saucepan. Add sugar and orange zest, bring to a boil, reduce heat to medium–low and boil until syrup is thick, about 10 minutes. Set aside.

In a frying pan over medium–low heat, heat 1 tablespoon ghee or oil. Add almonds and fry gently until golden. Remove from pan and set aside.

Heat remaining ghee or oil in frying pan, add chicken and brown. Move chicken to a plate, leaving fat in pan, and season with salt and pepper.

Add onion to frying pan and fry gently over medium–low heat until soft and slightly browned, about 10 minutes. Add 1 cup (8 fl oz/250 ml) water and stir to deglaze pan. Add chicken, cover and simmer for 10 minutes.

Bring 8 cups (64 fl oz/2 L) water to a boil in a large pot. Add rice and 1 tablespoon salt. Return to boil and cook for 8 minutes. Drain rice in a sieve or colander and turn into a bowl. Strain syrup from orange over rice, reserving zest. Preheat oven to 300°F (150°C/gas 2). Butter a large baking dish (casserole) and spread half of the rice in it.

Arrange chicken pieces and onion on top of rice. Add half the cooking liquid from chicken. Sprinkle with half the orange zest and almonds. Spread remaining rice on top, pour remaining chicken cooking liquid evenly over top, cover and cook for 40 minutes. Remove top layer of rice from dish and arrange around the edge of a warm serving platter. Remove chicken to a plate and place remaining rice in center of platter. Top with chicken pieces and garnish with remaining orange zest and almonds. Sprinkle with pistachio nuts. Pour saffron liquid over the rice around chicken.

**Serves 5 or 6**　　　　　　　　　　**Cooking time 1 hour**

## Ingredients

2 oranges

2 cups (16 fl oz/500 ml) water

1 cup (8 oz/250 g) granulated sugar

4 tablespoons ghee or oil

¹/₂ cup (2 oz/60 g) slivered blanched almonds

2 lb (1 kg) boneless chicken breasts, quartered

1 tablespoon salt, plus extra salt to taste

freshly ground black pepper

1 medium yellow (brown) onion, sliced

2 cups (14 oz/440 g) basmati rice

¹/₂ cup (1 oz/30 g) shelled, blanched pistachio nuts, chopped

¹/₂ teaspoon saffron threads, steeped in 2 tablespoons hot water for 10 minutes

## Ingredients

1½ lb (750 g) finely ground (minced) beef or lamb

1 clove garlic, crushed

1 small yellow (brown) onion, finely grated

2 thick slices stale white Italian bread, crusts removed

1 egg

1 teaspoon ground cumin

2 tablespoons finely chopped fresh flat-leaf (Italian) parsley

salt

freshly ground black pepper

all-purpose (plain) flour for coating

¼ cup (2 oz/60 g) butter or ¼ cup (2 fl oz/60 ml) olive oil

Rice Pilaf (page 102) for serving

TOMATO SAUCE

1½ cups (9 oz/280 g) chopped, peeled tomatoes

½ cup (2½ oz/75 g) finely chopped green bell pepper (capsicum)

½ teaspoon sugar

salt

freshly ground black pepper

½ cup (4 fl oz/125 ml) water

MEAT

# Meatballs in tomato sauce

## İzmir köftesı (Turkey)

In a bowl, combine beef or lamb with garlic and onion. Soak bread in cold water, squeeze dry and crumble into bowl. Add egg, cumin, parsley and salt and pepper to taste. Mix thoroughly to a smooth paste. With moistened hands, form 1 tablespoon portions of meat mixture into oval, sausagelike shapes. Coat lightly with flour.

Heat butter or oil in a deep frying pan over high heat, and fry meatballs until lightly browned on all sides. Remove to a plate.

To make tomato sauce, add tomatoes and bell pepper to frying pan and cook over medium heat for 5 minutes. Add sugar and salt and pepper to taste, then stir in water.

Bring sauce to a boil and return meatballs to pan. Reduce heat to low. Cover and simmer until meatballs are tender and sauce is thick, about 1 hour. Serve with Rice pilaf.

**Serves 5–6**
**Cooking time 1½ hours**

# Moussaka

## Moussaka (Cyprus)

Cut eggplant into slices 1/4 inch (6 mm) wide. Place in a colander, sprinkle with salt and leave for 30 minutes. Rinse and pat dry with paper towels. Cut zucchini lengthwise, then slice potatoes and zucchini the same width as eggplant.

In a large frying pan over high heat, pour in olive oil to cover the base of the pan. Beginning with potatoes and ending with eggplant, fry vegetables until lightly browned. Add more oil as needed. Drain vegetables on paper towels.

To make meat sauce, cook onion in the same pan over medium–low heat until translucent, about 8 minutes. Stir in garlic and cook for a few seconds. Add ground beef or lamb and cook over high heat, stirring often, until color changes. Add tomato puree, wine, parsley, sugar and cinnamon. Season with salt and pepper, cover and simmer on low heat for 30 minutes.

For béchamel sauce, melt butter in a heavy saucepan over medium–low heat. Stir in flour and cook for 2 minutes; do not allow to brown. Add milk all at once, stirring constantly, until milk comes to a boil. If sauce is lumpy, stir with a balloon whisk. Boil for 1 minute, then remove from heat. Stir in nutmeg, 1 tablespoon cheese, and salt and pepper to taste. Cover surface of sauce with plastic wrap if not using immediately.

Preheat oven to 350°F (180°C/gas 4). Place potato in a layer in the bottom of a greased 10 x 13-inch (25 x 33-cm) baking pan (oven dish). Spread with half the meat sauce and top with zucchini slices. Spread remaining meat sauce on top and cover with eggplant slices.

Stir eggs into béchamel sauce. Pour over eggplant, spreading evenly. Sprinkle on remaining cheese. Bake until tops are golden brown, 50 minutes. Stand 5 minutes before cutting into squares to serve.

**Serves 6**
**Cooking time 2 hours**

## Ingredients

1 lb (500 g) eggplant (aubergines), unpeeled

salt

1 lb (500 g) zucchini (courgettes), unpeeled

1 lb (500 g) potatoes, peeled

olive oil as needed

MEAT SAUCE

1 large yellow (brown) onion, finely chopped

2 cloves garlic, crushed

2 lb (1 kg) ground (minced) beef or lamb

1½ cups (12 fl oz/375 ml) tomato puree

¼ cup (2 fl oz/60 ml) dry red wine

3 tablespoons chopped fresh flat-leaf (Italian) parsley

1 teaspoon sugar

1 teaspoon ground cinnamon

salt

freshly ground black pepper

BÉCHAMEL SAUCE

¼ cup (2 oz/60 g) butter

⅓ cup (2 oz/60 g) all-purpose (plain) flour

2 cups (16 fl oz/500 ml) milk

¼ teaspoon ground nutmeg

⅓ cup (3 oz/90 g) grated Romano or Parmesan cheese

salt

freshly ground pepper

2 eggs, lightly beaten

## Ingredients

1 oz/30 g tamarind pulp

1 cup (8 fl oz/250 ml) warm water

5 large yellow (brown) onions, unpeeled

1½ lb (750 g) ground (minced) beef or lamb

½ cup (3½ oz/105 g) long-grain rice, rinsed

1½ teaspoons baharat (page 120)

½ teaspoon turmeric

salt

freshly ground black pepper

½ cup (2½ oz/75 g) chopped, peeled tomatoes

2 tablespoons tomato paste

2 tablespoons chopped parsley

1 tablespoon vegetable oil

1 tablespoon melted ghee or vegetable oil

2 teaspoons sugar

# Stuffed onions
## Basal mahshi (Gulf States)

In a small bowl, soak tamarind in half the warm water for 30 minutes. Strain into a bowl, pressing with back of spoon to separate pulp from liquid. Reserve liquid and discard seeds and fibers.

Peel onions and carefully cut out the root with the point of a knife. Slit onion on one side through to center, cutting from top to root end.

Bring a pot of water to a boil, add onions and boil until softened, 8–10 minutes. Drain and let cool.

In a bowl, thoroughly combine beef or lamb with rice, Baharat, turmeric, salt and pepper to taste, tomatoes, tomato paste, parsley and vegetable oil.

Carefully separate the onion layers. Outer layers may be cut in half; leave inner layers intact. Discard onion centers. Place about 1 tablespoon meat mixture on a layer of onion and roll up firmly.

Coat a heavy saucepan with ghee or oil. Place the rolls in pan with seam-side down. Sprinkle layers lightly with salt.

Combine tamarind liquid with remaining warm water and sugar. Pour over the rolls.

Invert a heavy plate on top of the rolls to keep them in place during cooking. Cover, bring to a simmer over medium heat, reduce heat to low and cook for 1½ hours. Serve hot with salads, pickles and pita bread. The onions may also be served at room temperature as an appetizer.

**Serves 6–8 as a main course, 12 as an appetizer**
**Cooking time 1¾ hours**

# Lamb **kebabs** with yogurt **marinade**

## Kabaub (Afghanistan)

Cut lamb into 1¼-inch (3-cm) cubes.

Combine yogurt, garlic, salt and a generous grinding of pepper in a glass or ceramic bowl. Add lamb cubes, stir to coat, cover and refrigerate for 4–5 hours or overnight (up to 12 hours).

Prepare a fire in a grill (barbecue), preferably charcoal. Thread five or six cubes of lamb on each of six metal skewers, leaving a little space between cubes. Brush off excess marinade, leaving a thin film.

If possible, set the skewers across the sides of the grill (barbecue) so meat is not directly on grill rack. Grill kebabs, turning them frequently until cooked to medium, about 10 minutes.

Remove cubes from each skewer and place on a pita bread half. Add tomato and onion slices. Fold bread to keep meat warm and serve immediately, garnished with lemon wedges and cilantro sprigs.

**Serves 6**
**Cooking time 15 minutes**

**Note:** If large pita breads are not available, use six small pita breads. Split open, but not in half, and fill with lamb, tomatoes and onions.

## Ingredients

1½ lb (750 g) boneless lamb shoulder

1 cup (8 oz/250 g) plain whole-milk yogurt

2 cloves garlic, crushed

1 teaspoon salt

freshly ground black pepper

3 large whole wheat (wholemeal) pita breads, split in half

sliced tomatoes

sliced yellow (brown) onions

lemon wedges for garnish

fresh cilantro (fresh coriander) sprigs for garnish

# Roast lamb

## Arni psito (Cyprus)

Preheat oven to 350°F (180°C/gas 4). Pat meat with paper towels. Cut slits all over surface of lamb. Cut garlic into slivers and insert into slits.

Season lamb with salt and pepper and place in a baking dish (roasting pan). Cook for 1 hour. Remove from oven and drain off fat.

Peel potatoes, halve lengthwise and cut part way down through the rounded side of each half. Place potatoes, rounded-side up, around lamb, and sprinkle with lemon juice, salt and pepper.

Top potatoes with onion slices, tomatoes and tomato puree. Add bay leaf and cinnamon stick, dot with butter and pour in stock or water and wine.

Return lamb to oven and cook for 1½ hours longer, turning lamb occasionally to brown evenly. An instant-read thermometer inserted into the thickest part of the lamb away from bone should read 150°F (65°C) for medium, 170°F (75°C) for well done.

Remove lamb to a carving platter, tent loosely with aluminum foil and let rest for 15 minutes. Skim excess fat from pan.

Carve lamb and serve with roast potatoes. Accompany with a tossed green salad or green vegetables.

**Serves 6**
**Cooking time 2–2½ hours**

**Note:** In Cyprus, lamb is cooked to well-done. If medium lamb is preferred, cook for 30 minutes at step 2. Medium-rare lamb is unsuitable for this dish.

## Ingredients

1 leg of lamb, about 4 lb (2 kg)

2 cloves garlic

salt

freshly ground black pepper

2 lb (1 kg) medium potatoes

juice of ½ lemon

2 large yellow (brown) onions, sliced

1½ cups (9 oz/280 g) chopped, peeled tomatoes

½ cup (4 fl oz/125 ml) tomato puree

1 bay leaf

cinnamon stick, about 3 inches (8 cm) long

2 tablespoons butter

½ cup (4 fl oz/125 ml) lamb or chicken stock or water

¼ cup (2 fl oz/60 ml) red or white wine

## Ingredients

6 lamb shoulder chops, about
   1¼ inches (3 cm) thick

¼ cup (2 oz/60 g) butter or ¼ cup
   (2 fl oz/60 ml) corn oil

1 large yellow (brown) onion, finely
   chopped

1 cup (8 fl oz/250 ml) tomato puree

1 cup (6 oz/185 g) chopped, peeled
   tomatoes

3 cloves

cinnamon stick, about 3 inches
   (8 cm) long

salt

freshly ground black pepper

4–5 cups (32–36 fl oz/1–1.25 L) boiling
   water or lamb stock

2 cups (14 oz/440 g) orzo (risoni)

¼ cup (1 oz/30 g) grated parmesan
   or romano cheese

½ cup (2½ oz/75 g) diced feta or
   haloumy cheese

# Lamb **chops** **with** pasta
## Yiouvetsi (Cyprus)

Preheat oven to 350°F (180°C/gas 4).

Place lamb in one layer in a deep baking dish (roasting pan). Spread butter on or pour oil over chops. Place in oven and cook for 20 minutes.

Remove from oven and evenly sprinkle onion over chops. Return lamb to oven and cook for 10 minutes longer.

Remove from oven and add tomato puree, chopped tomatoes, cloves, cinnamon stick and salt and pepper to taste. Baste chops with liquid in pan. Return lamb to oven and cook until meat is tender, about 1 hour; add a small amount of boiling water or stock if needed to keep the meat moist.

Add remaining boiling water or stock to pan and stir in pasta. Cook, stirring occasionally, until pasta is tender, about 20 minutes. Add water if the contents of the pan look dry.

Remove from oven, sprinkle cheeses over pasta and return to oven for 5 minutes. Serve immediately.

**Serves 6**
**Cooking time 2 hours**

# Lamb with dried fruit

## Hamuth heloo (Iraq)

Cut lamb into ³/₄-inch (2-cm) cubes. Heat half of the ghee or oil in a heavy saucepan over high heat. Add lamb and cook, turning as needed, until browned on all sides, 8–10 minutes.

Push meat to one side, add onion and cook for 5 minutes. Reduce heat to low and add 1 cup (8 fl oz/250 ml) water, salt to taste, cinnamon stick and dried lime (pierced twice with a skewer) or lemon zest. Cover and simmer 45 minutes.

Place chopped dates in a small pan with remaining 1 cup (8 fl oz/250 ml) water. Set over low heat until dates soften. Press through a sieve into a bowl to puree.

Add date puree, apricots, prunes, raisins and brown sugar to pan. Stir to combine, cover tightly and simmer until lamb is tender, about 1 hour. Add more water during this time if the meat and fruit seem dry.

Remove cinnamon and dried lime or lemon zest and discard. Serve lamb with Rice Pilaf.

**Serves 5–6**
**Cooking time 2 hours**

**Note:** When dates are being dried, they exude a thick syrup resembling molasses. Iraqi cooks add some of the syrup to this dish. Soaked and pureed, dried dates with brown sugar added, provide a similar flavor.

## Ingredients

2 lb (1 kg) boneless lamb shoulder

¹/₄ cup (2 oz/60 g) ghee or ¹/₄ cup (2 fl oz/60 ml) vegetable oil

1 medium yellow (brown) onion, chopped

2 cups (16 fl oz/500 ml) water

salt

small piece cinnamon stick

1 dried lime or zest from ¹/₂ lemon

¹/₂ cup (3 oz/90 g) chopped pitted dates

³/₄ cup (4 oz/125 g) dried apricots

³/₄ cup (4 oz/125 g) dried prunes, pitted

¹/₄ cup (1¹/₂ oz/45 g) golden raisins (sultanas)

2 tablespoons brown sugar

Rice Pilaf (page 102) for serving

## Ingredients

¼ cup (2 oz/60 g) clarified butter or ghee or ¼ cup (2 fl oz/60 ml) olive oil

2 medium yellow (brown) onions, finely chopped

¼ cup (1 oz/30 g) pine nuts, plus pine nuts for garnish, optional

8 oz (250 g) coarsely ground (minced) lamb or veal

¼ teaspoon ground cinnamon

salt

freshly ground black pepper

1 recipe Kibbe (page 80)

¾ cup (6 fl oz/180 ml) melted clarified butter or olive oil

2 tablespoons cold water

# Baked kibbe

## Kibbeh bil sanieh

### (Lebanon, Syria, Jordan)

Warm butter or oil in a frying pan over medium–low heat. Add onions and cook until translucent, about 7 minutes. Add pine nuts and lightly brown, about 5 minutes.

Raise heat to high and add ground lamb or veal. Cook, stirring frequently, until juices evaporate and meat begins to brown, about 6 minutes. Remove from heat, and add cinnamon and salt and pepper to taste.

Prepare kibbe but do not chill unless making it in advance.

Preheat oven to 350°F (180°C/gas 4). Brush an 11 x 13-inch (28 x 33-cm) baking dish (roasting pan) or a 14-inch (35-cm) round baking dish (roasting pan) with butter, ghee or oil.

Press slightly less than half of the kibbe onto the bottom of the dish, smoothing it with a spatula. Top with ground meat mixture, spreading evenly. Dot with mounds of remaining kibbe, then carefully press out evenly so meat filling stays in place. Smooth top with spatula.

Run a knife blade around the edge of the dish, then deeply score the kibbe into diamond shapes. Press a pine nut into the center of each diamond if desired. In a measuring cup, combine melted butter, ghee or oil with cold water and pour over the kibbe, making sure some runs between the sides of the dish and the kibbe.

Bake until firm to touch, about 30 minutes. To brown top, sprinkle lightly with water three or four times during cooking. Cut through scored diamonds. Serve hot or cold with yogurt, salads and pita bread.

**Serves 6–10**

**Cooking time 45 minutes**

**Note:** Use olive oil rather than clarified butter or ghee, if serving cold. Baked Kibbe may also be cooked without filling. Spread evenly in dish, score as required and pour on melted butter or oil before baking.

## Ingredients

12 medium-size ripe tomatoes

½ teaspoon sugar

salt

freshly ground black pepper

6 tablespoons olive oil

1 large yellow (brown) onion, chopped

¼ cup (1½ oz/45 g) pine nuts, optional

1½ cups (10 oz/300 g) medium-grain rice

½ cup (3 oz/90 g) dried currants

1½ cups (12 fl oz/375 ml) hot water

2 tablespoons chopped fresh flat-leaf (Italian) parsley

2 tablespoons chopped fresh mint

water or dry white wine as needed

# Stuffed **tomatoes**
## Tomates yemistes (Cyprus)

Slice top from each tomato and reserve. Scoop out pulp with a spoon and set aside.

Put pulp in a saucepan with sugar and salt and pepper to taste. Simmer over low heat until soft, about 10 minutes. Press the pulp through a sieve into a bowl and reserve puree.

Heat 3 tablespoons oil in a frying pan over medium–low heat. Add onion and fry until translucent, about 5 minutes. Add pine nuts if used and cook for 5 minutes longer.

Stir in rice, currants, hot water, parsley and mint. Season to taste with salt and pepper. Bring to a boil, cover, reduce heat to low and simmer until liquid is absorbed, about 10 minutes.

Preheat oven to 350°F (180°C/gas 4). Fill tomatoes with rice mixture, allowing room for rice to expand. Replace tops and arrange stuffed tomatoes in a baking dish (roasting pan).

Pour pureed tomato and an equal quantity of water or white wine into dish. Drizzle remaining oil over tomatoes. Bake, uncovered, until rice is tender, about 30 minutes. Serve hot or cold.

**Serves 4–6**
**Cooking time 50 minutes**

**Note:** This makes a pleasant lunch dish or an attractive accompaniment to main dishes.

## Ingredients

8 medium Japanese (long) eggplants (aubergines)

3 medium yellow (brown) onions

6 tablespoons olive oil

4 cloves garlic, chopped

3 medium tomatoes, peeled and chopped

3 tablespoons chopped fresh flat-leaf (Italian) parsley

salt

freshly ground black pepper

2 tablespoons lemon juice

pinch of sugar

½ cup (4 fl oz/125 ml) water

# Stuffed **eggplants**

## Imam bayildi (Turkey)

Remove stems from eggplants or leave intact if desired. At intervals along the length of each eggplant, peel off strips of skin, ½-inch (1-cm) wide, to create a striped effect. Cut a deep lengthwise slit on one side of each eggplant, without cutting all the way through the eggplant, stopping short of the ends.

Slice each onion lengthwise, then cut into slender wedges. In a large frying pan over medium–low heat, heat 3 tablespoons oil. Add onion and fry until translucent, about 8 minutes. Add garlic and cook for 1 minute. Place onions and garlic in a bowl and combine with chopped tomatoes, parsley and salt and pepper to taste.

Heat remaining 3 tablespoons oil in the same pan over high heat. Add eggplants and fry until lightly browned on all sides but still rather firm, about 10 minutes. Remove pan from heat and turn eggplants slit-side up.

Spoon vegetable mixture into slits, forcing in as much filling as possible. Spread remaining filling on top. Add lemon juice, sugar and water to pan and cover tightly. Cook over low heat until eggplants are tender, about 45 minutes. Add more water only if the liquid in the pan evaporates.

Let cool to room temperature and serve as an appetizer or a light meal with bread, or as a salad accompaniment.

**Serves 4–8**
**Cooking time 1¼ hours**

# Green **beans in oil**

## Lubyi bi zayt (Lebanon, Syria, Jordan)

Trim beans and remove strings if necessary. Cut into 2-inch (5-cm) lengths or slit lengthwise.

Heat olive oil in a frying pan over medium–low heat. Add onion and fry until translucent, about 8 minutes. Add garlic and cook for a few seconds longer.

Add tomatoes, tomato paste, water, sugar and salt and pepper to taste. Cover and simmer until tomatoes are soft, about 15 minutes.

Add beans and parsley; cover and simmer until beans are tender, 15–20 minutes. Serve hot, or at room temperature as is traditional.

**Serves 6**
**Cooking time 45 minutes**

### Ingredients

1 lb (500 g) green beans

¼ cup (2 fl oz/60 ml) olive oil

1 medium yellow (brown) onion, chopped

2 cloves garlic, chopped

1 cup (6 oz/185 g) chopped, peeled tomatoes

1 tablespoon tomato paste

½ cup (4 fl oz/125 ml) water

½ teaspoon sugar

salt

freshly ground black pepper

2 tablespoons chopped fresh flat-leaf (Italian) parsley

# Baked mixed vegetables

## Güveç (Turkey)

Remove stems from eggplants. At intervals along the length of each eggplant, peel off strips of skin, $1/2$ inch (1 cm) wide, to create a striped effect. Cut Japanese eggplants into $1/2$-inch (1-cm) slices; quarter globe eggplant lengthwise, then cut into chunks. If using globe eggplant, spread pieces on a baking sheet and sprinkle liberally with salt. Let stand for 30 minutes, then pat dry with paper towels.

Heat 3 tablespoons oil in a frying pan over high heat. Add eggplant and fry until lightly browned, 8–10 minutes. Remove to a plate – do not drain.

Heat remaining 3 tablespoons oil in same pan over medium–low heat. Add onions and fry until translucent, about 5 minutes. Stir in garlic, cook for 1 minute, then remove from heat.

Preheat oven to 350°F (180°C/gas 4). Place a layer of eggplant in the bottom of an 8-cup (64 fl oz/2 L) capacity, baking dish (casserole). Top with some zucchini, bell peppers and green beans. Spread some onion mixture on top and cover with tomato slices. Sprinkle with salt, pepper and some of the parsley. Repeat layers until all ingredients are used, reserving some tomato slices and parsley.

Top with okra if using, cover with reserved tomato slices, and sprinkle with reserved parsley. Season with salt and pepper and add water.

Cover and bake until vegetables are tender, 1–1$1/2$ hours. Serve as an accompaniment to roast or grilled (broiled) meats and poultry. Can also be served as a light meal; bread and feta cheese are customary accompaniments.

**Serves 6**
**Cooking time 2–2$1/2$ hours**

## Ingredients

2 Japanese (long) eggplants (aubergines) or 1 medium globe eggplant

salt

6 tablespoons olive oil

3 small yellow (brown) onions, sliced

2 cloves garlic, crushed

4 small zucchini (courgettes), cut into 1$1/2$-inch (4-cm) pieces

3 small green bell peppers (capsicums), seeded and quartered

8 oz (250 g) green beans, trimmed

4 or 5 small tomatoes, peeled and sliced

freshly ground black pepper

3 tablespoons chopped fresh flat-leaf (Italian) parsley

8 oz (250 g) okra (see page 85), optional

$1/2$ cup (4 fl oz/125 ml) water

## Ingredients

1½ cups (10 oz/300 g) dried chickpeas (garbanzo beans)

4 cups (32 fl oz/1 L) cold water

⅓ cup (3 fl oz/90 ml) olive oil

1 large yellow (brown) onion, chopped

2 cloves garlic, chopped

¼ cup (2 oz/60 g) tomato paste

2 tablespoons chopped fresh flat-leaf (Italian) parsley

1 tablespoon chopped fresh mint

1 teaspoon ground cumin

1 teaspoon sugar

salt

freshly ground black pepper

1½ lb (750 g) spinach

extra-virgin olive oil for serving

# Chickpeas with spinach

## Nivik (Armenia)

## and Nohutlu ispanak (Turkey)

Put chickpeas in a bowl, add water and let soak in a cool place for 8–10 hours or overnight.

Drain chickpeas and rinse well. Place in a large saucepan with fresh water to cover. Bring to a boil, cover and cook over low heat until tender, 1–1½ hours.

Heat oil in a frying pan over medium–low heat. Add onion and cook until translucent, about 7 minutes. Add garlic and cook for a few seconds. Stir in tomato paste, parsley, mint, cumin, sugar and salt and black pepper to taste. Add to chickpeas, cover and simmer for 10 minutes.

Remove any attached roots and damaged leaves from spinach and discard. Wash spinach leaves and stems well in several changes of water. Drain, then coarsely chop leaves and stems. Add to chickpeas, stir well and simmer, uncovered, until spinach is cooked, about 10 minutes. Mixture should be moist, but not too liquid.

Serve hot or at room temperature. Add extra-virgin olive oil to taste.

**Serves 6**
**Cooking time 1½–2 hours**

# Cabbage rolls

## Mihshi malfuf

### (Lebanon, Syria, Jordan)

To make meat filling, heat clarified butter or oil in a frying pan over medium–low heat. Add onion and fry until soft, about 7 minutes. Place in a bowl with lamb or beef and remaining filling ingredients. Mix well to combine.

To make chickpea filling, heat olive oil in a frying pan over medium–low heat. Add scallions and fry until soft, 2–3 minutes. Place in a bowl and add to remaining filling ingredients. Mix well to combine.

Core cabbage and place whole in a large pot of boiling salted water. Cook just long enough to soften leaves, about 10 minutes. Drain in a colander and cool under cold running water. Carefully remove the leaves.

Cut thick ribs from larger leaves, then halve the leaves; keep smaller leaves intact. You will need 24 leaves. Use ribs and trimmings to line a deep saucepan.

Using chosen filling, place a generous tablespoon at the base of each leaf, roll one turn and tuck in sides to contain filling. Roll firmly to end of leaf.

In a small bowl, mix garlic, mint, lemon juice and a small amount of salt. For chickpea-filled rolls, beat in oil. Pack the rolls, seam-side down, in lined pan, sprinkling some garlic-lemon mixture on each layer of rolls.

Invert a heavy plate directly on the rolls to keep them in place during cooking. Pour in stock (for meat-filled rolls) or water (for chickpea-filled rolls) to just cover the rolls. Cover pan tightly with lid.

Bring to a boil over medium heat, reduce heat to low and simmer for 1 hour for meat filling or 45 minutes for chickpea filling. Serve meat-filled rolls hot or warm; let chickpea-filled rolls stand in the pan for 30 minutes and serve lukewarm or cold. Serve with yogurt on the side and pita bread.

**Serves 6**
**Cooking time 1–1¼ hours**

## Ingredients

**MEAT FILLING**

2 tablespoons clarified butter or olive oil

1 medium yellow (brown) onion, finely chopped

1½ lb (750 g) ground (minced) lamb or beef

½ cup (3 ½ oz/110 g) long-grain rice

½ teaspoon ground allspice

salt

freshly ground black pepper

¼ cup (2 fl oz/60 ml) water

**CHICKPEA FILLING**

¼ cup (2 fl oz/60 ml) olive oil

8 scallions (shallots/spring onions), chopped

1 cup (7 oz/220 g) long-grain rice

1 cup (6 oz/185 g) drained, canned chickpeas (garbanzo beans)

6 tablespoons finely chopped fresh flat-leaf (Italian) parsley

1 cup (6 oz/185 g) chopped, peeled tomatoes

½ teaspoon ground allspice

salt

freshly ground black pepper

**CABBAGE ROLLS**

1 medium head cabbage

4 cloves garlic, finely chopped

2 tablespoons chopped fresh mint or 2 teaspoons dried mint

¼ cup (2 fl oz/60 ml) lemon juice

¼ cup (2 fl oz/60 ml) olive oil (for chickpea-filled rolls)

2 cups (16 fl oz/500 ml) chicken stock or water

plain whole-milk yogurt for serving

pita bread for serving

## Ingredients

2 cups (14 oz/440 g) long-grain rice

¼ cup (2 oz/60 g) butter

2 cups (10 oz/300 g) coarsely grated carrots

½ teaspoon whole black peppercorns

1 teaspoon sugar

3½ cups (28 fl oz/875 ml) chicken stock

salt

# Turkistan **carrot** pilaf

## Türkistan pilavı (Turkey)

Place rice in a fine-mesh sieve and rinse under cold running water until water runs clear. Drain well.

Heat butter in a heavy saucepan over medium heat. Add carrots and peppercorns and fry, stirring often, until hot, about 3 minutes. Sprinkle with sugar toward end of frying.

Add rice and cook, stirring constantly, for 2 minutes.

Pour in stock and add salt to taste. Bring to a boil, stirring occasionally, then reduce heat to low. Cover and cook until rice is tender, about 20 minutes.

Remove from heat, place a kitchen towel or two paper towels over the rim of the pan, replace the lid, and let pilaf stand for 5 minutes before serving. This pilaf is excellent with roast chicken.

**Serves 5–6**
**Cooking time 30 minutes**

## Ingredients

¼ cup (2 fl oz/60 ml) corn oil or
¼ cup (2 oz/60 g) butter

1 medium yellow (brown) onion,
finely chopped

3¼ cups (26 fl oz/810 ml) chicken
stock or water

2 cups (12 oz/375 g) coarse bulgur
(burghul)

salt

plain whole-milk yogurt for serving

# Bulgur pilaf
## Pourgouri pilafi (Cyprus)

In a saucepan over medium–low heat, heat oil or butter. Add onion, cook until translucent, about 7 minutes. Add stock or water and bring to a boil.

Place bulgur in a fine-mesh sieve and rinse quickly under cold running water. Pour into boiling liquid, adding salt to taste. Bring to a boil, stirring constantly, then reduce heat to low. Cover and cook until liquid is absorbed, about 20 minutes.

Remove from heat, place a kitchen towel or two paper towels over the rim of the pan, replace lid, and let pilaf stand for 15 minutes before serving. Serve with yogurt as an accompaniment to mixed vegetable dishes or any dish normally served with rice pilaf.

**Serves 6**
**Cooking time 45 minutes**

# Rice pilaf
## Beyaz pilav (Turkey)

Place rice in a fine-mesh sieve. Rinse under cold running water until water runs clear, and drain well.

Heat butter in a heavy saucepan over medium heat. Add rice and cook, stirring constantly, for 5 minutes.

Pour in stock and add salt to taste. Bring to a boil, stir occasionally, then reduce heat to low. Cover with lid and cook until rice is tender but firm to the bite, about 20 minutes.

**Serves 6**
**Cooking time 30 minutes**

## Ingredients

2 cups (14 oz/440 g) long-grain rice

½ cup (2 oz/60 g) butter

3½ cups (28 fl oz/875 ml) chicken
stock

salt to taste

# Steamed rice

## Chelou (Iran)

### Ingredients

8 cups (64 fl oz/2 L) water

2 cups (14 oz/440 g) basmati rice

2 tablespoons salt

1/4 cup (2 oz/60 g) butter or ghee

1/4 cup (2 fl oz/60 ml) water

Bring water to a boil in a large, heavy saucepan. Add rice and salt and bring to a boil, stirring occasionally. Cook for 5 minutes, then pour immediately into a large sieve and drain.

In a small saucepan, heat butter or ghee with 1/4 cup (2 fl oz/60 ml) water until bubbling. Pour half of the mixture into the saucepan which was used to boil rice, and swirl the pan to coat the bottom and sides.

Spread half the rice in base of pan. Add remainder of rice on top in a mound and make a deep hole in the centre with the handle of a wooden spoon. Pour remaining butter or ghee mixture over the top.

Cover rim of pan with a doubled kitchen towel or two paper towels, and place lid on firmly. Cook rice over medium–low heat for 10 minutes, then reduce heat to low and cook for 35 minutes longer.

**Serves 6**                    **Cooking time 50 minutes**

# Variation
## Steamed Crusty Rice
## Chelou ta dig (Iran)

Follow basic recipe for steamed rice to stage where pan is coated with butter mixture. Mix about a cup of the rice with an egg yolk or 1/4 cup (2 oz/60g) plain whole-milk yogurt. Spread in the bottom of pan, mound remaining rice, make hole and pour on remainder of butter mixture.

Cover pan as above and cook over medium heat for 15 minutes, then reduce heat to medium-low and cook for 30 minutes longer. By this time, bottom of rice should be golden brown and crisp.

Place pan on a cool surface, such as a kitchen sink, for a few minutes to loosen rice from pan. Spoon top layer of rice into a heated serving dish. Break crusty layer into pieces and arrange, browned-side up, around rice.

## Ingredients

- 2 cups (14 oz/440 g) basmati or other long-grain rice
- ½ teaspoon saffron threads
- 2 tablespoons rosewater
- 5 tablespoons (3 oz/90 g) ghee or ⅓ cup (3 fl oz/90 ml) vegetable oil
- ¼ cup (1 oz/30 g) halved blanched almonds
- 1 medium yellow (brown) onion, finely chopped
- 8 oz (250 g) ground (minced) lamb or beef
- ½ teaspoon baharat (page 120) or ground allspice
- ½ teaspoon salt, plus extra salt to taste
- ¼ cup (1½ oz/45 g) golden raisins (sultanas)
- 3 cups (24 fl oz/750 ml) chicken stock

# Saffron rice

## Timman z'affaran (Iraq)

Place rice in a fine-mesh sieve and rinse under cold running water until water runs clear. Place in a bowl, add cold water to cover and let soak for 30 minutes.

Place saffron in a mortar and pound with a pestle. Place in a small bowl, add rosewater and set aside to steep.

Heat 2½ tablespoons ghee or oil in a frying pan over medium–low heat. Add almonds and fry until golden, about 5 minutes. Remove to a plate with a slotted spoon.

Add onion to the same pan and fry until translucent, about 7 minutes. Raise heat to medium–high and add lamb or beef. Cook, stirring often, until the meat is crumbly and juices evaporate, about 10 minutes. Add Baharat, ½ teaspoon salt and raisins and fry for 1 minute longer. Remove from heat, cover and set aside.

Heat remaining 2½ tablespoons ghee or oil in a deep, heavy saucepan over high heat. Add 2 teaspoons saffron mixture and chicken stock. Bring to a boil.

Drain rice and add to boiling stock with salt to taste. Bring to a boil, stirring occasionally, then reduce heat to low. Cover pan tightly and cook until rice is just tender, about 20 minutes.

Fold meat mixture gently through rice, place a kitchen towel or two paper towels over the rim of the pan, replace the lid and continue to cook over low heat for 5 minutes. Remove from heat and let the rice stand for 5 minutes before serving.

Spoon rice in a serving dish or onto a platter. Sprinkle with fried almonds and remainder of saffron mixture. This rice is excellent served with roast chicken or lamb, or as part of a buffet.

**Serves 5–6**
**Cooking time 50 minutes**

# Rice with onion

## Mashkoul (Gulf States)

### Ingredients

2 cups (14 oz/440 g) basmati or other long-grain rice

6 cups (48 fl oz/1.5 L) cold water

1 tablespoon salt

1/4 cup (2 oz/60 g) ghee or 1/2 cup (2 fl oz/60 ml) vegetable oil

1 large yellow (brown) onion, finely chopped

Place rice in a fine-mesh sieve and rinse under cold running water until water runs clear. Drain well.

Bring water to a boil in a large saucepan, add rice and salt and return to a boil, stirring occasionally. Cook for 8 minutes, then immediately drain in a large sieve.

Heat ghee or oil in a heavy saucepan over medium–low heat. Add onion and fry until translucent, about 7 minutes. Raise the heat to medium–high, and fry onion until crisp and lightly colored, about 7 minutes longer. Remove half of the onion and ghee or butter to a small bowl and set aside.

Add rice to saucepan and toss with a fork to combine with onion. Put reserved onion on top of rice. Cover pan tightly and cook over low heat until rice is tender, 35–40 minutes. Fluff with a fork and serve piled on a platter. Rice with Onion is a standard accompaniment to most Gulf States dishes.

**Serves 5–6**
**Cooking time 1 hour**

## Ingredients

1 lb (500 g) dried figs

4 cups (32 fl oz/1 L) cold water

⅓ cup (2 oz/60 g) whole blanched almonds

¾ cup (6 oz/185 g) granulated sugar

thin strip lemon zest

juice of 1 lemon

3 tablespoons honey

chopped almonds, pistachios or walnuts for garnish

whipped cream or plain whole-milk yogurt for garnish

# Figs in syrup

## İncir kompostosu (Turkey)

Rinse figs well, place in a bowl and add cold water. Let stand for 8 hours until plump. Drain off water into a heavy saucepan.

Insert an almond into each fig from bottom. Set aside.

Add sugar to water in pan and cook over medium heat, stirring occasionally, until sugar dissolves. Add lemon zest, juice and honey, and bring to a boil.

Add stuffed figs and return to a boil. Reduce heat to low and cook, uncovered, until figs are tender and syrup is thick, about 30 minutes. Remove lemon zest and discard.

Arrange figs upright in a bowl. Pour syrup over figs, let cool, cover, and chill in refrigerator.

Sprinkle with chopped nuts and serve with whipped cream or yogurt.

**Serves 6–8**
**Cooking time 45 minutes**

# Almond cream **pudding**

## Muhallabia (Lebanon, Syria, Jordan)

In a small bowl, mix ground rice in $^1/_4$ cup (2 fl oz/60 ml) milk. Bring remaining milk to a boil in a heavy saucepan. Stir in ground rice mixture, salt and sugar.

Reduce heat to medium and cook, stirring constantly with a wooden spoon, until mixture bubbles gently. Reduce heat to low and simmer for 5 minutes, stirring often so mixture cooks slowly and does not scorch.

Stir in ground almonds until blended smoothly, then add rosewater. Remove from heat and stir occasionally until mixture cools slightly.

Pour into a serving bowl or six individual small bowls.

Chill in refrigerator and serve garnished with chopped nuts, and with pomegranate seeds if desired.

**Serves 6**
**Cooking time 15 minutes**

### Ingredients

3 tablespoons ground rice

3 cups (24 fl oz/750 ml) milk

pinch of salt

$^1/_4$ cup (2 oz/60 g) sugar

$^3/_4$ cup (3 oz/90 g) ground blanched almonds

1 tablespoon rosewater

chopped pistachios or almonds for garnish

pomegranate seeds, optional

## Ingredients

2½ cups (12½ oz/390 g) all-purpose (plain) flour

½ teaspoon ground mahlab, optional

¼ cup (2 fl oz/60 ml) melted butter

⅓ cup (3 fl oz/90 ml) milk

¼ cup (2 oz/60 g) granulated sugar

¼ cup (2 fl oz/60 ml) olive or walnut oil

confectioners' (icing) sugar, optional

DATE FILLING

8 oz (250 g) pitted dates

¼ cup (2 oz/60 g) butter

1 teaspoon rosewater

# Date **crescents**
## Sambusik (Lebanon, Syria, Jordan)

Sift flour into a bowl with mahlab, if using. Add butter and, using your fingers, rub into flour until evenly distributed.

In a small saucepan over low heat, warm milk and sugar, stirring until sugar is dissolved. Let cool to lukewarm.

Pour milk into flour. Add oil and mix until a soft dough forms. Knead in bowl until smooth.

To make date filling, chop dates and put in a saucepan with butter. Place over medium heat and stir until mixture is combined and pastelike in consistency. Remove from heat and stir in rosewater.

Preheat oven to 350°F (180°C/gas 4).

Roll out dough on a lightly floured work surface until ¼ inch (5 mm) thick. Use a 2-inch (5-cm) cookie cutter to cut dough into rounds.

Place a heaped teaspoon of date filling in center of each round. Fold dough over filling to form a crescent. Crimp edge using your fingers or press with tines of a fork to seal.

Place crescents on ungreased baking sheets and bake until lightly colored, 20–25 minutes. Let cool on sheets for 5 minutes, then place on a wire rack to cool completely. Alternatively, dust crescents with sifted confectioners' sugar while hot. Store crescents in a sealed container for up to one week.

**Makes 30**
**Cooking time 30 minutes**

# Shortbread cookies

## Ghiraybah (Gulf States)

### Ingredients

1 cup (8 oz/250 g) clarified butter or ghee

1 cup (8 oz/250 g) confectioners' (icing) sugar, sifted

2½ cups (12 1/2 oz/390 g) all-purpose (plain) flour, sifted

Chill clarified butter if it is too soft. Put butter or ghee in a bowl and beat until light. Gradually add sugar, beating until mixture is very creamy and light.

Fold flour into butter mixture. Knead lightly in bowl until smooth. If kitchen is hot, chill dough in refrigerator 1–2 hours.

Preheat oven to 325°F (170°C/gas 3).

Roll pieces of dough into walnut-sized balls and place on ungreased baking sheets. Press a floured thumb into center of each ball to make a dimple and to flatten dough slightly.

Bake until cookies are very lightly colored and almost firm, 20–25 minutes. Let cool on baking sheets until firm. Remove and store in an airtight container. These cookies are delicate and must be handled carefully. They will keep for one week.

**Makes 35–40 cookies**
**Cooking time 20–25 minutes**

**Note:** These cookies are prepared in most Middle Eastern countries. Sometimes they are topped with a blanched almond or pine nut instead of being dimpled; others are finished with a dusting of confectioners' (icing) sugar.

## Ingredients

1 lb (500 g) phyllo

¾ cup (6 fl oz/180 ml) melted clarified butter

½ cup (2 ½ oz/75 g) chopped pistachio nuts, optional

NUT FILLING

2 egg whites

½ cup (3 ½ oz/105 g) superfine (caster) sugar

2 cups (10 oz/300 g) coarsely ground walnuts

2 cups (10 oz/300 g) coarsely ground, blanched almonds

1 teaspoon rosewater

'ATAR SYRUP

2 cups (1 lb/500 g) granulated sugar

1½ cups (12 fl oz/375 ml) water

1 teaspoon lemon juice

1 teaspoon orange flower water

1 teaspoon rosewater

**Note:** If you are not used to working with phyllo, it is advisable to fill and shape the first batch of buttered squares before going on to the next batch. The butter firms fairly quickly, making the pastries difficult to shape if the buttered sheets are left too long.

# Nut pastries

## Baklawa 'be'aj'

### (Lebanon, Syria, Jordan)

Prepare, stack and butter phyllo as directed on page 21, using 10 sheets in each stack.

Using kitchen scissors, cut each stack into 4-inch (10-cm) squares. Set aside and cover. Prepare remainder of phyllo sheets following the same process. Depending on the size of the phyllo, you may have fewer than 10 left at the end. Halve sheets if necessary to give 10 layers.

Preheat oven to 325°F (170°C/gas 3). Butter a 10 x 13-inch (25 x 33-cm) metal baking dish (roasting pan).

To make nut filling, beat egg whites in a bowl until stiff. Gradually beat in sugar. Fold in walnuts, almonds and rosewater.

Butter top of phyllo square and place 1 heaped tablespoon nut filling in the center. Gently squeeze into a lily shape, with the four corners of the square like petals loosely enclosing the filling. Repeat with remaining phyllo squares and filling. As they are shaped, place finished pastries close together in the prepared dish.

Bake for 30 minutes, then reduce oven temperature to 300°F (150°C/gas 2) and bake until golden, about 15 minutes longer, taking care that the nut filling does not burn.

Meanwhile, to make 'atar syrup, dissolve sugar in water in a medium saucepan over medium–low heat, stirring occasionally. Add lemon juice and orange flower water, and bring to a boil. Boil until syrup is the consistency of thin honey, about 15 minutes. Stir in rosewater and let cool.

Spoon syrup over hot pastries. Let cool and sprinkle pistachio nuts in centers of pastries, if desired.

**Makes about 40 pastries**
**Cooking time 45 minutes**

# **Almond** baklava

## Baqlawa (Iran)

In a bowl, combine ground and chopped almonds with sugar and cardamom.

Preheat oven to 325°F (170°C/gas 3). Brush a 10 x 13-inch (25 x 33-cm) metal baking dish (roasting pan) with some of the clarified butter or ghee.

Place three sheets phyllo in prepared dish, brushing each sheet with butter or ghee. Brush the top sheet with butter or ghee and sprinkle on one-third of nut mixture. Top with two more sheets, brushing each with butter or ghee.

Repeat with another two layers of nut mixture, layering between them two sheets of phyllo brushed with butter or ghee. Top the last layer of nuts with three sheets of phyllo, brushing each with butter or ghee.

Trim edges of phyllo with a sharp knife. Carefully cut through layers to create diamond shapes (see page 21), spacing the cuts 1¼ inches (3 cm) apart. Pour remaining butter over top, letting it run into cuts and around sides. Sprinkle the top lightly with cold water to prevent the phyllo from curling during baking.

Bake on center rack of oven until phyllo is pale gold, 35–40 minutes.

Meanwhile, to prepare syrup, place sugar and water in a heavy saucepan. Cook over medium heat, stirring occasionally, until sugar is dissolved. Bring to a boil, add lemon juice and cardamom, and boil rapidly until the syrup is the consistency of thin honey, 15–18 minutes. Add rosewater, remove from heat, and set aside.

Pour warm syrup evenly over hot pastry. Let stand for at least 2 hours before cutting again and removing from dish. Pastry may be left in dish and covered lightly with a kitchen towel. It will remain crisp for 3–4 days. Do not refrigerate.

**Makes about 40 pieces**
**Cooking time 35–40 minutes**

## Ingredients

3 cups (12 oz/375 g) ground blanched almonds

1 cup (5 oz/150 g) finely chopped blanched almonds

1 cup (7 oz/220 g) superfine (caster) sugar

1 teaspoon ground cardamom

¾ cup (6 fl oz/180 ml) melted clarified butter or ghee

10 sheets phyllo

SYRUP

2 cups (16 oz/500 g) granulated sugar

1½ cups (12 fl oz/375 ml) water

1 teaspoon lemon juice

½ teaspoon ground cardamom

1 tablespoon rosewater

**Note:** For best flavor, purchase cardamom pods and process to a powder in a mortar with a pestle – or make sure that your source of already-ground spices sells quality products.

# Guide to weights and measures

The conversions given in the recipes in this book are approximate. Whichever system you use, remember to follow it consistently, thereby ensuring that the proportions are consistent throughout a recipe.

## WEIGHTS

| Imperial | Metric |
|---|---|
| ⅓ oz | 10 g |
| ½ oz | 15 g |
| ¾ oz | 20 g |
| 1 oz | 30 g |
| 2 oz | 60 g |
| 3 oz | 90 g |
| 4 oz (¼ lb) | 125 g |
| 5 oz (⅓ lb) | 150 g |
| 6 oz | 180 g |
| 7 oz | 220 g |
| 8 oz (½ lb) | 250 g |
| 9 oz | 280 g |
| 10 oz | 300 g |
| 11 oz | 330 g |
| 12 oz (¾ lb) | 375 g |
| 16 oz (1 lb) | 500 g |
| 2 lb | 1 kg |
| 3 lb | 1.5 kg |
| 4 lb | 2 kg |

## VOLUME

| Imperial | Metric | Cup |
|---|---|---|
| 1 fl oz | 30 ml | |
| 2 fl oz | 60 ml | ¼ |
| 3 fl oz | 90 ml | ⅓ |
| 4 fl oz | 125 ml | ½ |
| 5 fl oz | 150 ml | ⅔ |
| 6 fl oz | 180 ml | ¾ |
| 8 fl oz | 250 ml | 1 |
| 10 fl oz | 300 ml | 1¼ |
| 12 fl oz | 375 ml | 1½ |
| 13 fl oz | 400 ml | 1⅔ |
| 14 fl oz | 440 ml | 1¾ |
| 16 fl oz | 500 ml | 2 |
| 24 fl oz | 750 ml | 3 |
| 32 fl oz | 1 L | 4 |

## USEFUL CONVERSIONS

| | |
|---|---|
| ¼ teaspoon | 1.25 ml |
| ½ teaspoon | 2.5 ml |
| 1 teaspoon | 5 ml |
| 1 Australian tablespoon | 20 ml (4 teaspoons) |
| 1 UK/US tablespoon | 15 ml (3 teaspoons) |

## Butter/Shortening

| | | |
|---|---|---|
| 1 tablespoon | ½ oz | 15 g |
| 1½ tablespoons | ¾ oz | 20 g |
| 2 tablespoons | 1 oz | 30 g |
| 3 tablespoons | 1 ½ oz | 45 g |

## OVEN TEMPERATURE GUIDE

The Celsius (°C) and Fahrenheit (°F) temperatures in this chart apply to most electric ovens. Decrease by 25°F or 10°C for a gas oven or refer to the manufacturer's temperature guide. For temperatures below 325°F (160°C), do not decrease the given temperature.

| Oven description | °C | °F | Gas Mark |
|---|---|---|---|
| Cool | 110 | 225 | ¼ |
| | 130 | 250 | ½ |
| Very slow | 140 | 275 | 1 |
| | 150 | 300 | 2 |
| Slow | 170 | 325 | 3 |
| Moderate | 180 | 350 | 4 |
| | 190 | 375 | 5 |
| Moderately Hot | 200 | 400 | 6 |
| Fairly Hot | 220 | 425 | 7 |
| Hot | 230 | 450 | 8 |
| Very Hot | 240 | 475 | 9 |
| Extremely Hot | 250 | 500 | 10 |